I0817599

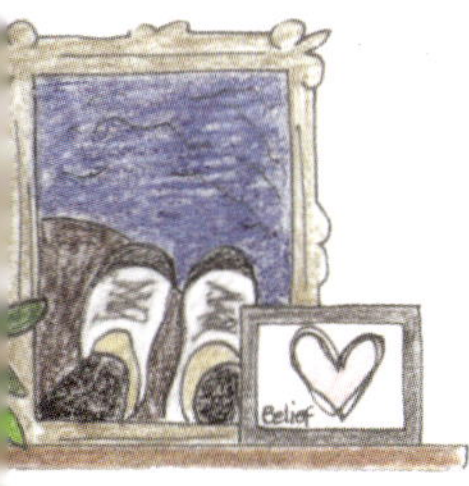

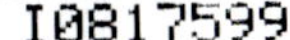

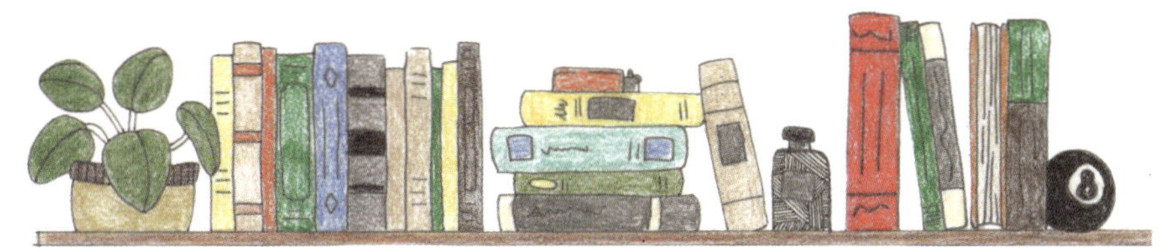

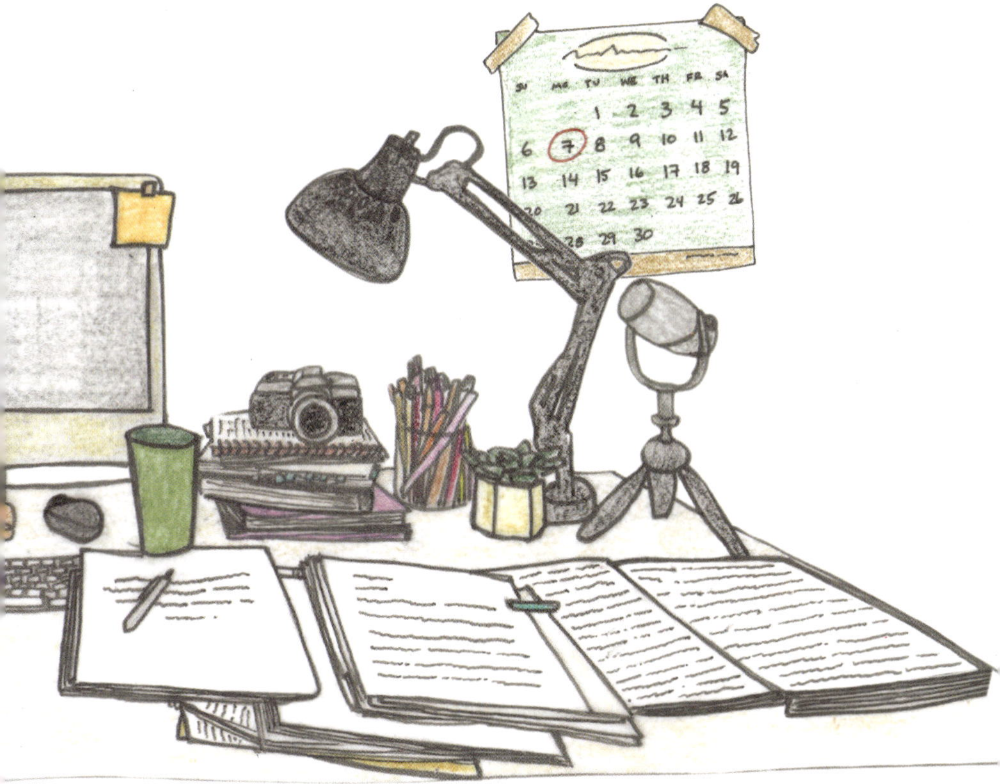
SU MO TU WE TH FR SA
1 2 3 4 5
6 7 8 9 10 11 12
13 14 15 16 17 18 19
20 21 22 23 24 25 26
28 29 30

That's a
great question,
I'd love to
tell you

That's a great question, I'd love to tell you

WRITTEN AND ILLUSTRATED BY

ELYSE MYERS

wm

WILLIAM MORROW

An Imprint of HarperCollins*Publishers*

HarperCollins books may be purchased for educational, business, or sales promotional use. For information, please email the Special Markets Department at SPsales@harpercollins.com.

hc.com

FIRST EDITION

Designed by Nancy Singer
Illustrations by Elyse Myers

Library of Congress Cataloging-in-Publication Data has been applied for.

ISBN 978-0-06-338130-8

Printed in Canada

26 27 28 29 30 TC 10 9 8 7 6 5 4

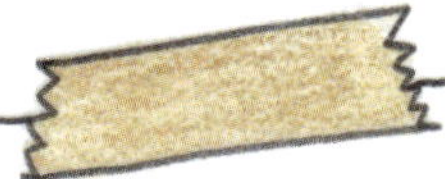

The stories you're about to read are true. I've done my best to capture them honestly, though memories (like a copy of a copy) tend to evolve over time. These pages include characters from my life whom I love, people I don't like at all, and many in between. Some characters are composites of a few different people in my life. Some names, dates, and details have been adjusted out of love, respect, and a dash of self-preservation to protect everyone's privacy. If you recognize yourself in these stories, congrats—you're unforgettable! (Or maybe you're not, and the resemblance you're spotting is purely coincidental.) Either way, enjoy!

♡e

For JONAS:

You are home to me.
Thank you for believing in me
enough for the both of us.

For AUGUST + OLIVER:

I love you more than you will ever know.
I hope you think this is cool.

For THIRTEEN-YEAR-OLD ELYSE:

I'm finishing what you started.
You are a <u>writer</u>!

Contents

How to Fold Hospital Corners in 10 EASY STEPS! 157
Everything She's Ever Wanted (to say but only remembers when she's angry and taking a shower) 171
House Clothes 178
Is This Enough Space? 199
The Rules on Face Touching: As It Relates to Surprise Facial Hair 193
My Very Last First Kiss 219
Cows, On Purpose. 227
To whom it will never concern, 237
Maybe I Will 241
A Very Short Novel (& Its Sequel) 258
Gratitude 267

May 25, 2017

I'm not quite sure when it started, this urgent desire to change everything about my life every so often. An uninvited sadness moves into my chest and grows. Day and night, it grows. Without my permission, it grows. Eventually, it becomes so large and untamed there isn't room for anything else, and I have no other choice but to admit it exists. I allow it to convince me that running away will make me feel better.

Any place will do.
Just as long as it isn't HERE.

THE DOOR TO
CALIFORNIA

Lucy

Some kids have imaginary friends.

Some have stuffed animals and security blankets.

Some become best friends with Magic 8 Ball key chains named Lucy.

ANAHEIM, CALIFORNIA. 2002.

The sun has finally gone down in my cul-de-sac. I can see Disneyland's Halloween fireworks from my front porch. My mom is deciding which bedsheet she's willing to sacrifice for my last-minute Halloween costume: a Ghost, complete with eyeholes and a mouth drawn on with black marker.

I avoid costumes that require plastic face masks because California never gets cold enough to wear them without sweating five minutes into trick-or-treating. Pretending to be a Ghost is even worse than wearing a plastic face mask, so I'm not sure why I've agreed to this. It's like wearing a light blanket all night. Fabric lying on top of my whole body, trapping all my heat and warm breath.

So much more sweat than a face mask.

Way more sweat than I'm comfortable with.

I throw the sheet over my head, and my mom quickly marks where she needs to cut so I'm able to see where I'm walking tonight. The first round of cuts is just for practice—those holes go in the back near the bottom so no one sees them. The second round of cuts is hopefully the last. If we need to do a third round of cuts, I think we'll have to sacrifice another sheet.

Am I a Ghost?

Am I a slice of Swiss Cheese?

Yes.

I will be whatever people think I am.

But mostly, I will be warm.

It's funny how much time I spend thinking about how to avoid overheating underneath this sheet when I probably won't spend more than ten minutes outside tonight. I don't like trick-or-treating, and my mom doesn't like Halloween. Something about it being Demonic? I'm not sure. I don't like Halloween, but for different reasons. All the decorations scare me, and ringing people's doorbells scares me more. This is why I never sell all my candy bars and wrapping paper when I take part in the fundraisers at school. My parents are my best customers because they have to be.

My friends Jessie and Nate like Halloween very much, and I like Jessie and Nate. They always have the *best* costumes. The ones that you buy specifically at a Halloween store that come in a sealed bag on a hanger. The kind that have photos of models wearing the costume showcased on the front of the package. We don't buy those costumes because my family is more of a DIY costume kind of family.

I always want a costume in a bag, but not enough to ask. There are always too many options, and I don't think I'd be able to make up my mind. I like seeing Jessie's and Nate's costumes every year.

My three older brothers' costumes are usually a combination of the same few choices: The Cowboy, The Ninja, The Sweatshirt And Jeans Paired With A Horrifying Mask That Gives Me Nightmares Until Christmas. Because they're much older than me, they have already been picked up by their friends and driven to a larger, fancier neighborhood that's known for passing out king-size candy bars. I'm slipping my SpongeBob Pillowcase off my bed and preparing for my night collecting as many fun-size Twix as I possibly can before I get too hot and ask to go home.

Deep breath in.

Deep breath out.

Princess Peach and Indiana Jones meet me at my front door and the night begins.

"Trick or treat!"

Each doorbell gets a little easier to ring. By the third or fourth house my friends and I have fallen into a comfortable rhythm.

Indiana Jones rings the doorbell and says hello. Princess Peach stands in front and talks about her sparkly pink dress made of tulle. I stand in the back and say nothing at all.

My purpose is to be the third person in our group and nothing else.

I am a *Ghost*, after all.

A Ghost or Swiss Cheese.

Neither of which does much talking.

If anyone asks, I can say I'm staying in character. I like this role very much.

When it comes time, I hold my pillowcase open and empty my mind so I feel thankful for whatever candy is thrown in. The harder I wish for Twix, the further the candy gets from Twix. When I start seeing Jolly Ranchers and off-brand Mike and Ikes, I stop wishing for anything at all.

I hope one of these houses has chocolate.

Maybe Twix, I don't know.

Maybe Twix.

I know any pieces of candy that are unmarked or unsealed are bound to be taken into my mother's custody at the end of the night. I write those off as soon as they're tossed into my pillowcase. Mom always asks my brothers and me to dump our candy onto the floor of the living room so she can inspect everything we receive. Part of her reasoning is the usual search for suspicious-looking candy that might contain tiny razor blades or poison or maybe both. Probably both.

"We should always be suspicious of *everyone*," she says. "You never know what someone might drop in your bag. You could be drugged! Do you want to be *drugged*?"

I really do not want to be drugged.

I'm happy to surrender all my Potentially Sharp and Poisoned Candy to her at the end of the night.

The other part is that she's also scanning our candy for the pieces she wants to take for herself. Mom Tax, she calls it. People don't really like when adults ask other adults for free candy, so Mom Tax seems like an excellent loophole. Especially for adults who are afraid to enjoy Halloween because they think it's Demonic.

The three of us—Princess Peach, Indiana Jones, and The Ghost Made of Cheese—make our way to nearly every house on our block. Every house except one. My back is covered in sweat, and I have only *one* fun-size Twix to show for it.

I don't think the small versions of candy should be called fun size.

I think *more* candy is fun. Not less candy.

When we finally make it to the fire hydrant at the end of our street, we turn around and start walking home. Our neighborhood empties out onto a main road, and all our parents agreed to let us trick-or-treat alone if we promised to stay within our cul-de-sac. The house at the end of the street—the corner house—is *technically* equal parts cul-de-sac and main road. If we *want* to go up to that house and ring the doorbell, we're allowed to. Technically.

If we want to.

But we've never wanted to.

Because the owners of the house on the corner that's equal parts cul-de-sac and main road like to dress their house up with decorations that look straight out of the horror movies my brothers watch without my mom knowing. This house always has a theme, and it's different every year.

And every year, the decorations get scarier.

And every year, I tell myself: *One day, I'm going to go up to their front door and ring their doorbell.*

And every year, I decide that next year is the year I'll finally try.

I hear they're known for giving out toys along with candy on Halloween.

I wonder if they have any Twix left.

"Hey, guys! Hold on," I yell after Princess Peach and Indiana Jones.

They've already started walking home, and I'm still standing in front of the scary house on the corner. I guess they hadn't noticed I wasn't walking with them. They look back.

"Do you dare me?" I point to the house that has been turned into a Haunted Circus just for tonight.

"No," Princess Peach says.

"You hate clowns," says Indiana Jones.

Neither of them sounds as excited or scared for me as I'd hoped they would. I don't think they really care whether I go ring the doorbell of this house.

I care very much.

Of all the years for me to finally feel brave enough to walk up to this house, it just had to be the year they chose clowns.

Clowns and weird red balloons and fog machines and fake blood oozing from a house that can't bleed.

"I'm going to do it. You guys wait here."

My friends look at each other. Indiana Jones takes off his hat and vest and sits down on the curb with his feet resting in the street. Princess Peach stays standing and picks up his candy-filled pillowcase from the ground. "That's gross. Don't put your candy on the ground."

They aren't paying attention to me at all.

"You promise you'll wait here for me?"

"We promise. Just hurry up."

I think Indiana Jones must be as warm as I am, and this reminds me of how much sweat I can feel dripping down my back.

I take one more look at the Haunted Circus in front of me, and I'm passed by a few older kids as they walk up the driveway, then up the porch steps toward the door. I borrow their confidence and follow them closely. Loud screams and haunting music are coming through hidden speakers somewhere behind all the fog.

If I can't hear anything, I think, *this might not be as scary.*

I test my theory. I cup my palms over my ears and press hard enough to dampen the sound of the screaming.

How can such nice people create something so *scary*?

I'm face-to-face with a clown with pitch-black eyes and a smile that doesn't look happy at all. I think this was a mistake. I think this was a very big mistake. I'm still pressing my hands against my ears when I try to turn around to go back down the driveway, but I end up slamming into a Witch and Pac-Man.

"Keep going!" Pac-Man shouts.

They hurry around me and say something to each other I can't hear.

I'm too far in—and too embarrassed to change my mind.

I keep going forward.

Up, up, up the porch steps.

Glowing eyes follow me through the front windows.

Big bags of kettle corn and—*oh my god, are those teeth?*—teeth line the porch and the front door. Someone else rings the doorbell so I don't have to.

At least there's that.

At least there's that.

A Ringmaster covered in blood answers the door. He's holding a top hat filled with candy and tips it toward the trick-or-treaters. Part of me (most of me) wants to ask someone in front to grab a handful of candy for me and pass it back.

But I think that would defeat the purpose of this whole thing.

And mostly, I don't think they would do it.

First the Witch, then Pac-Man.

It's finally my turn. I reach out and grab a handful of candy. I don't look to see what I'm grabbing because I don't want to look at anything at all. In fact, I want this entire night to be over so I can go home and never walk near this house again.

When the candy hits the bottom of my pillowcase, something makes a loud *clink!* that doesn't sound like the crinkle of plastic candy wrappers I've been hearing all night. Something harder.

Was it a necklace? Or maybe a bracelet?

All I want is a Twix.

"A trick with your treat!" says the Bloody Ringmaster.

I have no idea if he's talking to me or what that means. I'm already walking.

Down, down, down the steps.

Past the smiling clown that doesn't look happy.

Through the fog machine and haunted noises.

Back to the safety of my cul-de-sac, right where it meets the main road.

Princess Peach and Indiana Jones are both sitting on the curb, waiting for me.

"How did it go?" they ask at the same time. This makes them laugh.

"Fine. I'm ready to go home."

We walk toward the heart of the cul-de-sac, them in front and me behind.

I open my pillowcase to see what kind of candy I grabbed from the top hat. The first thing I see isn't candy at all. It's dark outside and the streetlights don't seem as bright as they usually are. My pillowcase is dark blue and doesn't allow much light through its fabric.

I reach in and grab it, whatever it is.

I'm holding a small Magic 8 Ball key chain.

"Did you get anything good?" Indiana Jones is looking more and more like Nate the closer we get to his house. He's taking off parts of his costume one by one until all that's left are his khaki pants and white t-shirt. The hat stays on.

"Nothing. It was dumb. Just a Reese's cup, I think."

"I'll trade you my Twix for your Reese's!" Princess Peach says. Her sparkly tulle dress is still very much on.

She doesn't look like she's sweating at all.

How is that possible?

We trade. I'm much less excited about my Twix than I should be.

All I can think about is my key chain.

I know if I say anything about the Magic 8 Ball, Nate and Jessie are going to say something to my mom out of excitement and the key chain will be taken from me before tonight is over.

I really don't want it to be taken from me.

There are certain rules in my house that keep me from consuming anything related to Magic, Witchcraft, and Things My Mom Calls Demonic.

It sounds like a fine-enough rule until you realize how many things my mom calls Demonic. This keeps me from watching things like *The Wizard of Oz* (mostly because of the flying monkeys, not the wizard) and reading books like Harry Potter. The *movies* were fine, I just wasn't allowed to read the books. One night a friend brought a Ouija board out at a sleepover. The number of times I was allowed back to that friend's house for sleepovers was exactly none more times.

But knowing I'm the proud owner of a Magic 8 Ball makes me feel like I just won the Secret Lottery.

I have no clue what I'm going to do with it.

Just owning it is enough for me to decide this is the best night of my life, so far.

The neighborhood porch lights have started to go dark. I don't know how all the parents decide it's time for the night to be over without talking to one another. Parents can do things like that: talk to each other without talking. I think it's a superpower parents get when they become parents.

Soon, I'll have to say good night to Nate and Jessie and empty all my candy out onto the living room floor. The closer I get to my house, the closer I feel like I am to losing my key chain.

I get quiet. I've been quiet the whole night, but now I am *silent*.

"Being Indiana Jones is...*itchy*!" Nate says.

He meets his parents at the top of his porch steps and flings his costume through the open front door. I can hear him complain to his parents about his overall Warmth and Itchiness. His voice follows him as he runs into the house. He throws us back a half wave without turning his head to say goodbye.

Jessie lives two houses down from Nate and eleven houses down from me, which means by the time Jessie and I are standing at the end of her driveway, the sidewalk leading up to my front door is almost visible to me through my shifting eyeholes. "I'll see you tomorrow, Jessie!" I say from under my sheet. Jessie tries to curtsy, but it looks more like she's trying to sit down Criss Cross Applesauce.

I would have usually taken the sheet off my head by now. I'm using it to buy myself some time so I can figure out what to do with this key chain.

How do I hide it?

Where do I hide it?

I like how safe I feel under this sheet.

I feel like I can keep all my secrets under here.

Secrets and lots of sweat and my key chain.

All of a sudden I am very aware of how tired my legs are from walking all night. My knees feel like they'll stop working all the way if I stand still for too long. I want to eat my candy, look at my key chain, and go to sleep without brushing my teeth.

I walk up to my front door and take off my shoes and socks

before walking inside. This is to protect everyone's nose. My feet are famously stinky. I find a good spot on the living room floor and begin the Candy Sorting process with my mom. I'm surrendering every piece of clear-wrapped candy to my mom, as well as a few individually wrapped pieces of Hershey's Dark Chocolate with Almonds. My mom is so focused on sifting through my Potentially Poisoned Candy that I'm able to slip my Magic 8 Ball into my palm and close my fingers around it. It's just small enough to hide if I hold my hand against my body *exactly* right.

I'm 90 percent sure this key chain isn't going to make it back into my bedroom with me, but I am 100 percent dedicated to the 10 percent chance that it might.

I palm the small black-and-white key chain like the magician I always knew I could be. To my surprise, I hide it so well that my mom completely misses it.

My candy has been thoroughly checked. I already know this candy is going to end up being hidden in my closet so that it "stays safe," and then I'll forget it exists. Before the words "You're good!" are done leaving my mom's mouth, I'm already standing up and running to my room.

"Thanksloveyougoodnight!"

Success.

"Aren't you forgetting something?"

I stop running.

My heart feels like it stops beating.

I turn around, expecting my mom to ask me for the Forbidden and Very Demonic Key Chain I'm hiding in my hand.

My mom is walking toward me with my pillowcase of candy in her hands.

Oh, the candy.

I forgot the candy.

I hide the key chain behind my back and grab the pillowcase from her. "Sorry. I got excited. Thanks."

I close my bedroom door behind me. I throw my stash onto my bed and jump up next to it. Holding my new key chain out in front of me, I start to think about all the answered Yes-or-No questions that are in my future.

"Does Nate like me—"

Start with something smaller. That's a big first question.

"Will I grow up to be a famous singer—"

What if the Magic 8 Ball can't see that far in advance?

"Will we have pizza for lunch tomorrow—"

You already know it's not pizza day tomorrow.

This is pointless.

I sit there for a very long time—maybe *forever*—trying to come up with the perfect first question. The longer I lie on my bed and think about it, the more pointless my potential questions start to feel. After a few more *forevers* and many questions being cut off in the middle, I give up.

I stare at my new magic friend. I feel like I'm letting it down in some way. Written in cursive along the front is the word "*LUCKY.*" I don't feel lucky right now; I feel like a very bad question asker.

I wonder if small things like this feel big to other people as well.

I hope if I open my journal and write everything down, maybe I'll come up with questions that feel perfect enough to ask out loud.

Dear Diary,

IF YOU'RE READING THIS AND YOU ARE NOT ELYSE JONES, STOP READING RIGHT NOW. I AM SERIOUS!

I have a secret. Are you ready? Really really ready?

I have a magic 8 ball keychain thing. The thing that has the answers in it. You ask it questions and it tells you your future. I don't know how it works. But I think it actually works. You can't tell my mom. If she knows I have a magic 8 ball, she is going to be really mad and take it. She will throw it away probably. I will have a funeral for the magic 8 ball if that happens. I am hiding it in my backpack. I am not going to tell anyone I have it. I got it from the scary house around the corner. It wasn't too scary just a little scary. i'm not scared of haunted houses and other scary things like that anymore. I still don't like scary movies but maybe I will one day. Nate and Jessie didn't get one because they were too scared of the house. I think Nate likes Jessie. Does Jessie like Nate? I don't want to ask her because I like Nate. The keychain is black and white and it has a long chain on the end and the chain is a silver metal color. Looks like this

I am going to name my magic 8 ball lucy because I like that name better than lucky and lucy is a cute name. I like it a lot. I am going to ask Lucy a question now and so I have to go. I will be right back and tell you about it. BYE!!!!

My journal has a lock on it that only two people have a key to: me (obviously) and my best friend, Elizabeth, who lives down the street from my grandma. She gave me the key to hers, but I lost it.

I still haven't told her.

My brain is still questionless. Maybe I should give Lucy to someone else so she isn't wasted. I hold the Magic 8 Ball in my sweaty hands and fall asleep wondering what it will be like to be at school tomorrow with a secret.

The school bell rings through the concrete hallways of my elementary school. The bells always surprise me.

I wonder if they'll ever stop surprising me.

Lucy and I make our way to Mrs. Keegan's room and I take a seat at my desk. Our desk.

Lucy, this is our desk now.

Lucy lives in my pencil box during the day, and I get to see her every time I reach for my eraser. All morning I've been hearing small whispers about a potential sleepover happening this weekend. I can hear people talking about it in class right now if I listen hard enough.

But I don't listen very hard, because I don't think I'm invited.

I don't know whose house the sleepover is at or whose mom to tell my mom to call. I'm not sad about not being invited. Sleepovers make me nervous. The blankets never smell like my blankets. I never know what to pack. The pajamas the girls wear are always the cute ones where the tops match the bottoms. Usually I end up having the parents call my parents to pick me up.

Sometimes I say, "I forgot something at home."

Sometimes I don't.

Sometimes my mom says it for me.

It's easier if I don't get invited. That means I don't have to forget anything at home. I feel someone behind me touch my shoulder. I turn around to see what my desk neighbor wants. She's holding out a folded-up note that looks like it's been passed through multiple sets of sticky elementary school hands.

To: Elyse

From: Sam

Samantha is the kind of friend I like talking to when I'm paired up with her as Line Buddies. She's not the kind of friend I talk to once school is over. I've never talked to her on the phone or been to her house.

I can't even picture her house or her mom.

Does she have brothers or sisters?

Has Samantha called herself Sam this entire time, and I just missed it?

This is exactly what I mean.

We're school friends and that's it. Jessie is my only friend who I regularly pass notes to in class. I know what *her* house looks like and I know her mom's name is Mrs. Mara. I go to Jessie's after school a lot, and I like being there. Her house is nice.

I've never been passed a note from anyone else besides Jessie.

This is new to me.

Why do I feel so afraid to open this note?

Before I can reach under my desk to grab my gel pen, Sam and I look at each other across the classroom. She's mouthing the words "OPEN IT" in combination with some impressive hand movements.

She looks like she's opening an invisible book.

I silently shout back, "OKAY," with two very large thumbs-up.

Maybe the double thumbs-up will make me look like I'm not nervous to open her note. I doubt it will, but that's fine.

I can feel my face get hot as Sam watches me read her note. Knowing she can see me reacting to what's written on the piece of paper makes my face feel even hotter. I wish I would have taken this to the bathroom and opened it up there.

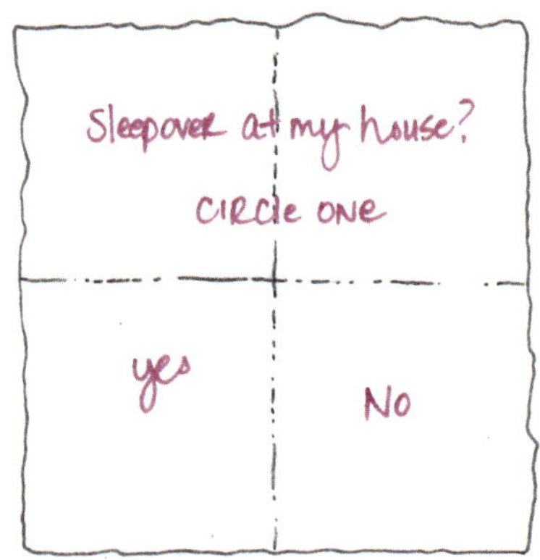

First: Is this a prank? Sam has never given me any reason to believe that she doesn't like me or wants to embarrass me. But things I don't expect to happen happen all the time. I have Lucy in my pencil box. I didn't expect *her*, so anything is possible.

Second: Do I even want to go to a sleepov—

"Is that something you'd like to read out loud? Or would you prefer I take it off your hands until after class?"

Mrs. Keegan's voice sounds suspiciously close to my desk.

She's whispering.

I whisper back: "You can keep it."

I think I'm happy Mrs. Keegan took that note from me. I wouldn't usually be glad a teacher took something from me in class, but right now I'm glad.

I wish something like a sleepover didn't make me this nervous. Why does it make me this nervous? It shouldn't. A sleepover should excite me.

I don't feel excited right now.

I feel a lot of things, but excitement is not one of them.

(When I grow up, I'll eventually discover what I'm feeling is anxiety, but for now, the best way to describe these feelings are: Fuzzy and Hot.)

When the lunch bell rings, I'm too embarrassed to walk up to Mrs. Keegan's desk at the front of the room and ask for Sam's note back. It's not that I'm afraid of getting into trouble if I go up there, because I don't think Mrs. Keegan was *that* upset by Sam and me passing notes. She puts up with Noah all day who sits three desks away from me and keeps threatening to let the class frog out of its tank if we're assigned any more silent reading.

We all put up with Noah.

I'm actually afraid of Mrs. Keegan's Superpowers:

1. Asking Questions
2. Mind Reading

She definitely can read my mind. I'm sure of it.

I don't want to tell her what Sam's note said (I don't think she'd actually ask) or why I froze when I read it (she's used to me freezing up). If I try to explain those two things to Mrs. Keegan, I'll also have to explain a bunch of other things as well, like: the fact that I wanted to check "No" because I'm afraid of new people and new things but I didn't want to check "No" because I didn't want Sam to think I don't like her and I also didn't want to check "Yes" because that would mean I'd have to go to the sleepover where there would be blankets that don't smell like my blankets at home but checking "Yes" would mean I get to go to a sleepover because I was invited to a sleepover.

My eyes are starting to burn as I stand at my desk, thinking about all that Explaining.

Lunch is too short to explain that many things.

I walk past Mrs. Keegan's desk, out of the classroom, and into the girls' bathroom.

Every single overhead light in here is working today. This never happens.

I spend as little time in this bathroom as possible because the lights are usually half on and half off. It makes this bathroom feel like a Haunted House.

I don't want to think about any more Haunted Houses.

There's something about a dark bathroom with flickering lights that really makes me question whether I have to go to the bathroom or not. Sometimes I think about the time Jessie and I played Bloody Mary in this bathroom, and I peed my pants because she lunged at me in the dark. She thought it was funny.

So did I, after a lot of time and a fresh set of clothes.

I actually didn't think it was very funny—then or now—but Jessie doesn't need to know that.

I lock myself in a well-lit stall and take Lucy out of my backpack.

"I finally know what I want to ask you," I say to Lucy as I hold her in one hand and hold the stall door closed with the other. The locks work just fine, but there's way too much space between the door and frame to trust them all the way. I hold the stall door closed just in case. "Should I sleep over at Sam's house this weekend?"

I close my eyes and shake Lucy as hard as I can. I realize as soon as I stop shaking her that she will *eventually* give me an answer, and there's a possibility her answer might be "Yes" in ten different flavors. My chances of getting "No" are half of that. I also have the chance of getting some version of "Ask Again" five different ways, which would put me back at the beginning.

Yes: ten.

No: five.

Maybe: five.

I've spent the last week writing down every possible answer

Lucy might give me, trying to prepare for the very first question I ask her.

Whenever I got around to it.

If I ever got around to it.

I regret knowing how likely I am to get a "Yes" from Lucy right now. I think I *want* to go to Sam's sleepover, but I know I'm scared. Why am I so scared?

Lucy, can you tell me why I'm so scared? Maybe one day, you'll talk back.

I shake Lucy for so long that when I stop shaking her I have to wait an entire minute—maybe it was ten minutes, maybe an hour—before the tiny bubbles of blue dye disappear enough for me to see Lucy's answer in the small window.

Did I accidentally scramble you, Lucy?

I hadn't felt very patient to begin with. Now I don't feel patient at all.

Fuzzy and hot and very impatient.

A few moments pass in this very bright bathroom, and I can finally make out a total of four words:

SIGNS POINT TO YES.

I want to try again.

"I should have asked you a pretend question!" I whisper to myself and Lucy in the bathroom stall. I had put so much thought into the first question I would ask Lucy that I hadn't considered the possibility of her answer letting me down.

I've made a key chain my friend. I've given her a name. I've carried her around with me for a week. If I don't listen to Lucy now, then what am I doing? I rip a piece of paper out of my notebook and grab the only pen I have in my backpack: a pink glitter gel pen that is a different shade of pink than Sam's.

I wonder if she'll notice.

I wonder if she'll care if she notices.

I re-create Sam's RSVP in my own handwriting. There's no way to hide the fact that this is a replacement note. If the different shade of pink doesn't give me away, the Winnie the Pooh notebook paper definitely will.

I hold Lucy in my left hand. I quickly write and then check "Yes" with my right hand.

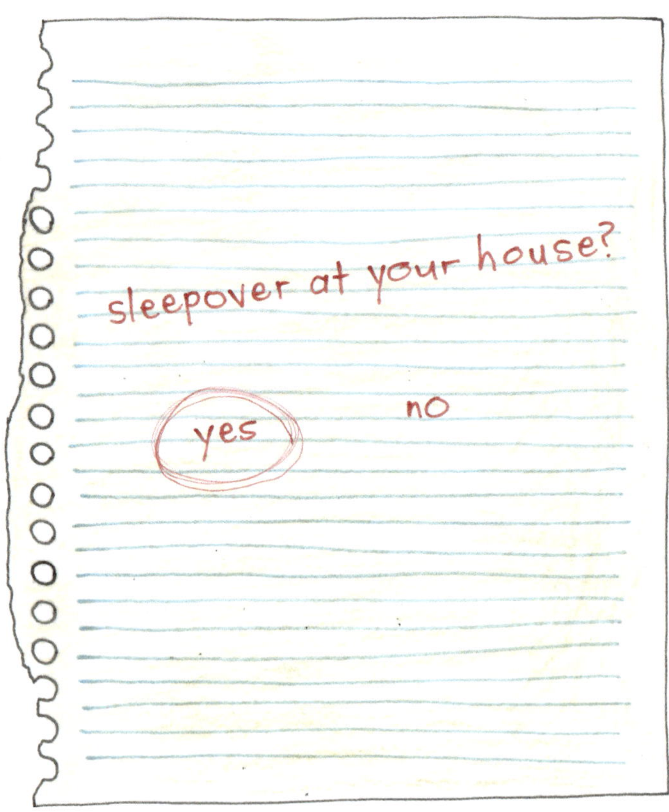

I fold the piece of paper in half three times. I shove the note into my pocket and walk out to the playground for the remaining eight minutes of lun—EIGHT MINUTES? Was I really in the bathroom for TWENTY-TWO MINUTES?

Lucy. We have to get faster at this.

I go looking for Sam while keeping a close eye on my Winnie the Pooh watch that I've worn on my left wrist every day since it was given to me two Christmases ago. I finally find her swinging on the monkey bars near the back of the playground. This search cost me an additional five lunch minutes. Since I like to be two minutes early to the class line (just in case), that leaves me with about thirty seconds to talk to Sam and thirty seconds to sprint back to the classroom line.

I stand on the ground underneath Sam as she transfers her weight back and forth between the same two monkey bars. I'm squinting as I look directly into the sun. I hold the folded note toward her. "My mom can call your mom. Thanks for inviting me."

Sam drops to the gravel and takes the note from me. "You probably shouldn't stand right under me when I'm on the monkey bars like that, you know. I could have kicked you in the face."

Sam laughs at the thought of kicking me in the face.

I'm not keeping a list of reasons For or Against this sleepover being a practical joke just to make me look stupid...but if I was? Sam laughing at the idea of accidentally kicking me in the face would definitely go in the "This Sleepover Is A Practical Joke Created To Make Elyse Look Stupid" column.

I'm just saying.

"Oh...kay. See you in class."

I tighten the straps of my backpack and check my watch again.

I like this watch so much.

I'm right on time.

I sprint back to our classroom's line-up spot, the sound of Lucy and a few other loose items shaking around in my mostly empty backpack as I run.

I stand first in line for Mrs. Keegan's class—two minutes early—and I think about what I just agreed to. I was so excited to ask Lucy my first question that everything else didn't have time to sink in until now.

I'm going to Sam's sleepover.

I was *invited* to Sam's sleepover.

I didn't know how badly I wanted Lucy to tell me "No" until she didn't.

She told me "Yes" and I listened.

I think I'm excited.

I think I'm excited that I'm excited.

I think I'm very scared.

Maybe more scared than excited.

Do I want to spend the night pretending I fit in with a group of girls who all know one another better than I know them? Not really. But going to Sam's sleepover because Lucy told me to go makes me feel a little less scared and a little more excited.

Not a *lot* less scared, but enough.

Maybe I'm allowed to go and feel uncomfortable the entire time.

Maybe being uncomfortable is okay?

Maybe I don't even have to pretend I'm not uncomfortable.

At the end of the day, I'm not the one who said "Yes."

Lucy said "Yes" *for* me.

seven

I'm not quite sure where Heaven is,

if Heaven is,

or what Heaven looks like,

But I doubt we'll find it in this closet. My back is against the bottom of a suit jacket that's hanging above us. I wish it would swallow me whole.

One Mississippi,

Two Mississippi,

Three Mississippi,

Four.

My knees are tight against my chest and my eyes are locked on to my worn white Chucks, which I refuse to replace. I'm sentimental about things that hardly matter, and I hold on to them longer than I'm meant to. Sometimes I wonder if I feel more emotional about inanimate objects than I do people. The sides are so worn down that only the inside lining of fabric is holding the sole in place.

I didn't consider until *right now* that maybe my shoes stink. Maybe it's an odor only others can smell, like the way the air in my house smells. I don't smell it at all because it's my house. Not a *bad* scent, but not a particularly good scent either. It is neither bad nor good, it only exists. And yet my nose still can't smell it because my nose lives in my house with the scent I can't smell.

Nose blind? Is that what it's called?
I wonder if that's a nose thing or a brain thing.
Maybe I need a vacation from my shoes.
Maybe Marley can smell my shoes.
Maybe I should finally let my mom buy me new shoes.
My mom will make me throw my old shoes away.
Maybe I should try washing these shoes first?
...Why am I so focused on my *shoes*?

My left wrist is ticking. It sounds louder than it did this morning. Can watches get louder? Is that possible? Only 360 Mississippis left. I hadn't realized how long a minute felt until I had to endure seven of them in a row.

I should say something.

I could tell him I'm claustrophobic? He already knows that, though. Besides, nothing kills a vibe faster than two people waiting for the inevitable onset of a panic attack.

Or a smell that might or might not (but probably might) exist.

Or the tick of a watch
that keeps getting *louder*.

I could say I need to throw up? If I'm looking to escape a room quickly—and without any questions asked—the threat of vomit would surely do it. That would *have* to work...right?

If I think about throwing up for too long, I won't even have to pretend!

I feel
uncomfortably
warm.

The walls are closer than they were ninety-seven Mississippis ago. I breathe out of my nose and swallow my saliva as a subconscious command to the contents of my stomach that they stay exactly where they belong. If anyone is out there listening to my thoughts, please keep all the vomit-related ones far away—pretend or otherwise. Maybe Grandpa John can hear my thoughts. Or maybe God? A god? All of them? Any of them will do.

I miss my grandpa.

Marley would know I was lying anyway. My mouth gives me away. The corners of my lips press so hard together they turn upward all on their own and my face ends up looking like a face trying to look like a face. He knows every single one of my tells, and he enjoys reminding me as often as he can.

Marley finds great joy in knowing me. To my surprise, I find equal joy in being known. I think that's the point of a friendship, isn't it? To be known? I must be doing something right, because I feel like I have a true friend in Marley. Maybe the truest. And being known isn't worth trading for a kiss.

I won't let myself lose a friend like him.

At this very moment, if I were the cup of Sprite I chugged just before being pushed into this closet, the liquid would be fear and the bubbles rising to the top would be joy. Yes, that's how I feel right now. Mostly fear, with joy floating through me, rising to the surface. Marley is the source of both.

If we aren't going to kiss, we might as well talk.

It *is* Marley, after all.

We've had plenty of conversations before this one, all lasting significantly longer than seven minutes. So why does every single one of these seven minutes feel so different? Heavy and upside down, like we're not just Marley and Elyse.

He doesn't feel like Marley at all right now. I wish he did. I'm sitting in front of a stranger. A stranger so close to me that if he were any closer, he would be sitting in my lap.

"If you could be in this closet with anyone tonight, who would it be?" I ask, because I've been to enough of these parties to know I'm not Marley's first choice. I'm not the second or third choice either. If Marley had a choice, I would still be standing in the kitchen with everyone else. Isabella would be the one silently fighting the bottom of Marley's hanging suit jacket. A suit jacket he most likely wears once every two years, to weddings and funerals.

Marley is a gentleman. Any Mississippi now, he'll switch sides with me and let my back rest against the door that separates us from everyone else while *he* pretends he's comfortable leaning against Nothing and Closet Air.

Air that's filled with wedding and funeral dust. *Oh god.*

How many funerals' worth of dust is floating around in this closet?

I've seen the inside of this coat closet only once, before tonight.

I don't own a coat nice enough to hang in this closet.

This closet's purpose is to house three things:

1. Perfectly Tailored Suit Jackets,
2. Things Made of Fur,
3. and Secret Kissing.

All three of which:
1. I have no experience at all.

"Are you asking because you really don't know? Or because you want me to say it out loud?"

I've already forgotten my question. Marley laughs, and the sound feels like a thermometer he's using to gauge the emotional temperature of the space around us. By now, my eyes have started to adjust to the dark, and I can see how nervous he looks sitting across from me.

Half Stranger,
Half Marley.

Oh, right. Yes. "I'm not an idiot, Marley. I'd imagine I'm low on your list of *'Top Ten People I'd Hope to Be Locked in a Closet With.'* It doesn't bother me, you know. We're friends. We'll always be friends."

"Why would you assume you aren't the first name on my list?"

"If I'm assuming anything, it's that I'm not on your list at all."

"You haven't seen my list, Elyse. My list could be a piece of paper with your name written on it ten times. What would you think about that?"

I think a *lot* of things about that. I don't have nearly enough courage or Mississippis to say any of it out loud. With nowhere else to go, an unexpected laugh exits my nose and I choke on my spit. Which makes me laugh harder.

Bubbles of Joy, rising to the top.
Floating through all the Fear.

I didn't realize I was holding my breath until I wasn't anymore. Almost fully adjusted to the lack of light, I look up to meet his eyes. I expected to see one of Marley's magic smiles that brighten his entire face. The closet needs it desperately. But he's looking at me, waiting impatiently for a response.

Did he just ask me a question?
Did I miss something?
I definitely feel like I'm missing something.

I rewind five Mississippis and press play in my head. *"My list... piece of paper...your name...ten times."* This is a joke. He made a joke...So why is he not laughing? Jokes are supposed to be funny. But this doesn't feel funny. Nothing about this interaction feels funny. And all I want is to make this feel funny. Funny feels safe.

I am Heavy Liquid.
Flat With No Bubbles.
He's a Stranger again.
No Marley.

"Sorry. I'm not laughing at you. It's just...I know you're doing me a favor by sitting in this closet with me."

I laugh when I'm nervous!

(is what I wanted to say.)

Laughing is what I do when I don't want to shake!

(is what I wanted to say next.)

But then Marley would ask why I'm nervous.

Which would require me to know why I'm nervous in the first place.

Which I obviously don't!
So please don't ask me!

"Th-thank you for…the way you reacted. Out there. When they threw us in here together. Tyler's party last week, well, you were there. It wasn't great. *This* is great. That *really* wasn't great. But this is great."

Do I really *not* know why I'm nervous?

I had a dream of being locked in a closet with Marley two nights ago. We skipped right past Polite and landed at His Lips Kissing My Lips. Dream Marley kissed me like he'd thought about kissing Dream Elyse many times before that.

I was definitely nervous when I woke up the next morning. Not because the dream scared me. I was nervous because it didn't scare me at all. Surely that has absolutely nothing to do with why I'm nervous right now.

In this closet.
The same closet that Dream Marley kissed Dream Elyse.
But just to be sure,
I won't mention it.
Ever.

Absolutely never.
Just to be safe.

"I'm not doing you a favor, Ely—"

"You could have asked to switch with someone else. With *anyone* else! Why didn't you ask Isabella to come in here with you? You...do like her, right? You can tell me, Marley. Do you like Isabella? When our time is up, you should tell her how you feel. I bet she likes you too. She would be silly not to. I've seen the way she looks at you. I can tell she likes you. Why are you smiling like that? What are you thinking—never mind, don't answer that. Answer the other things but not that last part. You should tell Izzy what you're thinking."

The Stranger Named Marley watches my lips as my words taper off into absolute nothingness.

My brain trusts my mouth
way more than it should.

Funeral Dust and Ghost Words,
and Other Memories Too Small To See.
There's not enough room in this closet for all of It and Us.

The steady flow of white noise and inner chatter finally stop escaping my mouth. I've returned it all into the folds of my brain, where it belongs. The look on his face tells me I'm scaring The Stranger Named Marley. Questions and statements interlaced with each other, thrown at him too quickly to properly respond to any of them. He responds to none.

Am I doing this on purpose?
Attempting to fill every pointless Mississippi with something else?

Something that isn't supposed to belong in this closet?

1. Suit Jackets,
2. Things Made of Fur,
3. and Secret Kissing.

~~Words.~~

"Isabella is...fine. But you think I want to be in here with Isabella? That's what you really think?"

I'm thinking so *many* things I wouldn't even know where to start.

I think Wi-Fi and Bluetooth feel like a mystery. Aliens are probably real, but we talk about the Zombie Apocalypse more. I'm probably breathing in bits of somebody's dead grandmother in here. I actually hate the taste of Sprite, but somehow the only other option at this party is Mountain Dew, which feels like the two most random drink options for people above the age of ten. I think Marley's parents have no idea their handle of vodka is going to be refilled with water tonight before it's shoved back into the cabinet above the fridge.

I think I wish I could travel back in time and redo the last four minutes, while simultaneously wishing the next three would hurry up and pass as quickly as possible. More quickly than possible.

But most of all, I think I want to be kissed by Marley.
And Marley wants to kiss Isabella.
I think that makes me sad.
I think it shouldn't.

There isn't a way to sufficiently summarize everything I'm thinking, and almost all my thoughts are irrelevant to the remaining one hundred and seventy-two Mississippis we have in this closet. Zombies don't interest Marley. Bringing up his dead grandmother feels like a terrible idea. He might be interested in the Sprite conversation, but—

"Of course that's what I think."

I said that too fast,
and I don't remember the question I just answered.

My left wrist has never been louder.
I wish tonight never happened.
I hope it happens again very soon.
I won't let it happen, but I hope nonetheless.
Something in Marley deflates right before me.

He is Marley again.
Not an ounce of Stranger left.
One complete and Wholly Familiar Marley.

His eyes fall from mine, and suddenly I feel like I'm in trouble. I've done something wrong. I'm not sure what, exactly. I couldn't have done anything wrong. Because I've done nothing at all. I've stuck to the script. I've delicately measured every single word, interaction, and accidental touch we've shared in this godforsaken closet to make sure it all adds up to the sum total of Completely Platonic.

"I thought maybe you felt…I just—I assumed you felt the same way I do."

My best friend.
My one and only friend.
I am so terrible at making friends.

I think I'll try to hold my breath for the last ninety Mississippis. I was a child in my grandmother's pool the last time I kept track of how long I could hold my breath underwater. But ninety feels like more Mississippis than I've ever held it before.

"The same?" I say, trying to let as little oxygen out of my lungs as possible.

I was right.
Ninety was way,
way too many Mississippis.
I think I might pass out.

Marley can read my mind. I'm absolutely sure of it. He will exit this closet and tell everyone I fell in love with him under the heat of the swinging light bulb that hangs above his mother's fur coats while he was busy planning his next seven minutes with Isabella.

Maybe I should wash my shoes when I get home,
and then change schools.

He looks shy. "I just thought we both felt the same way about each other."

I don't think a single one of our thoughts or feelings has been the same in this version of Heaven that, if I were to be pressed for an opinion, feels a little Hellish. I wasted two years and six and a half minutes convincing myself that I didn't want to be kissed by Marley. In the spirit of consistency, I am going to spend the next thirty Mississippis the exact same way.

"We're friends. We'll always be friends. That's what you mean, isn't it?"

"Elyse." His face is the most beautiful combination of serious and sorry. "No, that's not what I mean. Not even close." At any moment it looks as though he could break up with me. But lucky for me, there's nothing for him to break.

Yes, how lucky am I that there's nothing to break.
I'm overwhelmed with luck.
Friends. We'll always be friends.
My one friend.

Is Marley still my friend?

I want to reach out and touch his face. I have the sudden urge to hug Marley and hold on to him as tight as I possibly can. So tight that he won't float away. He feels like he's floating away. More than anything in the world, I want my arms to reach out in front of me and betray the limits my brain has placed on my body without my consent.

We're running out of time.
I wish my eyes would un-adjust.
I wish my wrist would stop *ticking*.

Four Mississippi,

We're both standing.
When did I stand up?

Three Mississippi,

I can see the sliver of light underneath the closet door disappear as the feet of his friends stand in front of it.

Two Mississippi,

"Then what do you mean?"
The question flies out of my mouth as a Hail Mary.
Rhetorical in every way.

One.

Sophie's Cigarette

I got close to smoking a cigarette once.
I chickened out at the very last second.

We are lying next to each other on the bed we constructed out of couch cushions, staring up at the ceiling as we talk. Sophie is sharing about her first Kiss With Tongue—an important distinction—with her brand-new boyfriend, Greg.

I'm word-vomiting about a boy who I'm convinced I'll marry.

(I'm just working up the courage to introduce myself to him first.)

Greg is older than us by three years. I can tell Sophie is proud she's dating a senior as a freshman, gauging by the sheer number of times she drops that information into her story. It sounds similar to a freshly engaged person learning how to casually drop the word "*fiancé*" into their first few post-engagement conversations.

There is nothing casual about it.

Greg smokes cigarettes. Sophie tried one. She hated it, and then smoked another. Greg gave her a pack of her own to keep if she ever wanted one while he wasn't around.

How romantic of him.

His gift now lives at the bottom of her underwear drawer, shoved into an empty box that was once home to a deck of cards.

"You have cigarettes? *Here?*" I shout out of pure shock. I'd forgotten where I was and the fact that it is practically midnight.

"Shhhhhhhutthefuckup, Elyse!" Sophie's hand flies over my mouth as she looks back toward her bedroom door. "That wasn't supposed to be a middle-of-the-night announcement to my entire *house*!"

Sophie smokes cigarettes.

Sophie *owns* cigarettes.

What else don't I know about Sophie? I suddenly felt jealous for the parts of her life she clearly doesn't feel safe enough to share with me.

Does she have any other hobbies I don't know about?

Does she smoke weed?

Does she have another best friend?

I'm hurting my own feelings with all these silent questions.

"Sophie, I'm so sorry, seriously. I didn't mean to yell. I just... I can't believe you smoke! I can't believe *I know* someone who smokes!"

My voice is now registering at an appropriate whisper, as if that somehow makes up for the information I'd broadcasted through the hallways and likely into her brother's and mom's bedrooms. I hold the blanket we were sharing over my head and giggle at the idea of Sophie owning something as forbidden as cigarettes.

"I don't know if I've ever even held a cigarette before. Does it hurt when you smoke? I feel like it has to hurt. I mean, it's gotta burn at least a little, right?"

Sophie shrugs nonchalantly. "I was thinking about going outside and having one anyway. Wanna come? You can try one if you want."

She is already to the point of smoking them casually?

All by herself?

Without Greg?

"I'm obviously coming with you. And I won't even scream

while going down the stairs." I put my hand up to my mouth and gesture like I'm locking up my lips and throwing away an invisible key. Sophie laughs, and I exhale freely with the relief of knowing she is no longer annoyed with me.

Sophie retrieves a box of playing cards from the bottom dresser drawer and tucks it into her sweatshirt pocket. With it, she also packs a lighter.

"Is the lighter a gift from Greg too?"

"What—this? No. I stole it from Cody. My brother has a million. He's constantly losing them. I think he buys a new one every time he smokes."

DOES EVERYONE SMOKE BUT ME?

WHEN DID I MISS THIS MEMO?

We make our way down the stairs, past the kitchen, over the puppy gates, through the living room, and out the front door without managing to step on a single squeaky toy.

Success.

We part from the paved path leading from Sophie's front door. We take a hard left through rosebushes to a small access road behind her house. There has to be another, less thorny way to get to this Magical Smoking Spot, but all right.

This is the only place Sophie is convinced she can safely stand without the smell of cigarette smoke wafting into her mom's ever-open bedroom window. I wonder if Sophie's mom smokes too.

Sophie is clumsy as she opens the box of playing cards that has been refurbished into a hiding place. She is even clumsier with the carton of cigarettes that hides inside. I don't claim to know much, if anything at all, about cigarettes. But the little I *do know* is that they aren't typically still wrapped in plastic if they've been opened and enjoyed.

A small part of me is relieved.

A *larger* part of me is worried about one of Sophie's neighbors seeing us, then ratting us out to Sophie's mom in the morning...but relief is definitely mixed in there.

Maybe my Best Friend is still my Best Friend. Maybe Sophie doesn't have other Secret Best Friends who are Secretly Cooler Than Me, who she Secretly Smokes With And Never Tells Me About.

Comfort washes over me as I watch Sophie peel off the protective plastic. She's as awkward with the pack of Marlboro Reds as any nonsmoker would be.

I'm still her Person!

Well...one of two Persons.

Because Greg and stuff.

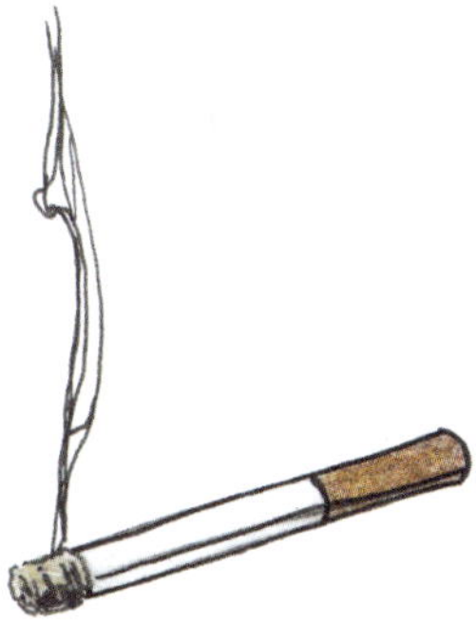

She handles the unlit cigarette between her fingers like a stage prop and lights the end of it with Cody's Lost Lighter.

One deep inhale and Sophie's face is immediately filled with pain.

The skin between her eyebrows bunches in a way I didn't know face skin could bunch. The lines around her mouth contort downward—so wildly that she looks more like a disgusted cartoon character than she does my Best Friend and Greg's Girlfriend Sophie.

Nothing about that deep breath of cigarette smoke looks enjoyable.

"You wanna try?" Sophie extends the burning embers toward me as she tries to paint a morsel of enjoyment onto her face. I think her Lying Face is intended for my benefit. But I'm almost positive it is helping her more than it's helping me. I wonder if smoking alone is as fun as smoking with Greg. She doesn't look like she's having fun at all.

But she likes Greg.

And Greg likes cigarettes.

Her visceral reaction to this secret hobby makes the next words out of my mouth very easy to say.

"Not even a little. I'm good."

I wrap the blanket I'd carried with me from her bedroom higher around my shoulders and take a deep breath. I'd never noticed how uncomplicated breathing felt until I watched someone willingly complicate it with hot cigarette smoke.

On purpose.

More than once.

I suddenly feel grateful for deep and uncomplicated breaths.

But to my surprise, I am infatuated by the smell. My mouth waters, and everything else in my brain goes silent. For a brief moment, my thoughts are vacuum-sealed and tightly packed away. I enjoy the temporary feeling of my own racing thoughts being none of my business—too far away to reach even if I need to get to them.

Looking down at my legs, I see small cuts from the rosebushes.

The vacuum seal is broken.

I wonder if I should ignore the cuts or ask for a Band-Aid.

While I stare at cuts that feel much deeper than they look, I make a silent promise to myself:

I will never tell a soul how much I like the smell of Sophie's cigarette.

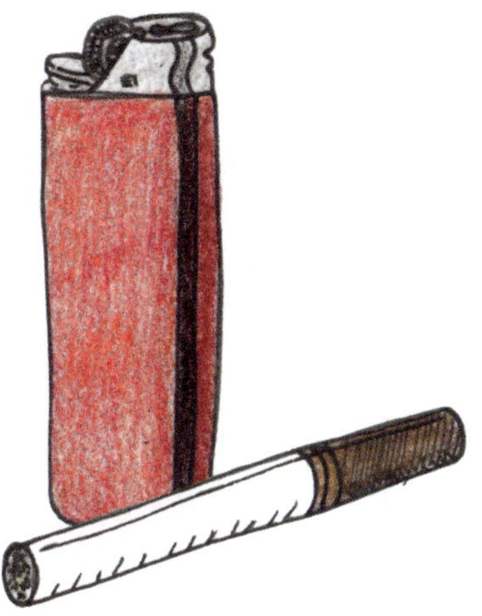

I have broken this promise many times.

Please Hold Your Questions Until the End

to be a child is to Believe, simply for Believing's sake.
to grow up is to Question.

(please hold your questions until the end.)

what a beautiful gift it is to be given a child's Belief. to be the person who owes a child Everything and, in return, is given a Belief so holy and limitless it sooner makes no sense than any sense at all. you are Everything You Say You Are, and you will do Everything You Say You Will Do. you will trade Everything for the expectation of Nothing and be rewarded with
pure,
and *wonderful,*
and *all-consuming,*
and *uninhibited,*
and *endless*
Belief!

some can't bear the uneven weight of such a trade.
but you can!
and you will!
because Belief is the only gift she can give you.
because you are the only one he wants to give It to.
because they will learn how to Believe by Believing you.
you can and you will because you *can*, so you *will*.

but can you?

she holds Belief in her hands and gives you more.

are you there?

you have so much Belief you don't know where to put it all.

will you keep It safe?

you're carrying her and all her Belief on your shoulders
when she feels herself start to slip.

are you steady?

she can't hold on to you and Belief at the same time,
so she lets go of Belief and holds on to you as tightly as she can.

what have you done with all her Belief?

maybe you aren't who she thought you were,
what you said you'd do,
where you said you'd be.
when you said you'd be.

did you say you'd be?
the person worthy of such
perfect,
and honest,
and brilliant,
and sacred
Belief?

you *didn't*,
and you *can't*,
and you *won't*.

so she will.

she takes back all her belief because you left it for her to find.
she's never seen Belief returned before,
and then you returned it.
so now she has.

how sweet is your relief from the burden of all her
suffocating,
and *relentless*,
and *time-consuming*,
and *unearned*
~~Belief?~~

she learned how to believe by Believing you.
belief is the only thing she can give you now.
and sometimes even belief feels like
too
much.

with all her Belief finally out of the way,
there is plenty of room for questions!
she'll go first.

Factory Reset

"Do you have a pen?" I feel someone's hot breath, reeking of coffee and weed, collide with the right side of my face.

"Excuse me?" I tilt my head toward the source of the smell and immediately regret my curiosity. The competing odors leaving this person's body are so pungent I can almost see them entering my field of vision, threatening to cling to me if I look toward them any longer.

I think my eyes are watering.

"I said...do you have a *pen*? I've watched you pull out, like, seventeen of them, all different colors, since I sat down three seconds ago. Can I *borrow one*?"

First of all, I don't have seventeen pens. I have *four*. And for the record, each serves a unique and important purpose. They are a part of an intricate color-coded note-taking system that I perfected over the summer. I don't have time to explain to him why each of these colors is important, especially when I can tell he already thinks my system is a waste of time without knowing it exists. If he assumes I'm going to sacrifice 25 percent of my system—an entire color—for someone who chronically walks in and takes a seat halfway through our lecture...

...then unfortunately he would be assuming correctly.

The only thing I hate more than forsaking a system I've decided is crucial to my success (and somehow the magic key to finally becoming organized and emotionally stable) is saying no to someone when they ask me for a favor.

"Hope you like blue." I extend my pen behind me, eyes locked on the PowerPoint at the front of the class.

I have no idea what's going on.

But *when* I figure it out, my pens are ready to document it.

Black is for general notes.

Green is for specific points I know will be important later.

Red is for questions I want to research when I have more time.

Blue is apparently for my neighbor who decided on a whim to join his nine o'clock architecture class without a backpack, notebook, or anything to write with.

A few minutes pass. I've almost recovered my spot in the textbook as it corresponds with the lesson that is actively being PowerPointed in front of me.

"You could get one of those four-in-one pens, you know."

Has someone taped a sign to me that says *TALK TO ME! ESPECIALLY WHEN YOU SHOULDN'T BE!* without my knowledge?

"But then what would I do when someone strolls into class, pen-less and late?" I'm facing forward in a useless attempt to remain focused. It takes a lot for my brain to lock in and unfortunately *very little* for my focus to be ripped away. The familiar sound of a plastic cap being crushed by someone's molars floats toward me, and I snap my head toward the sound.

"Are you *chewing* on my pen?"

He smiles as he lets the pen fall out of his hand and rest effortlessly in his mouth, tucked into the side of his cheek. Just three minutes ago it had been lying in my pencil case.

Where it belongs.

Right now.

Perfectly unchewed by a stranger's teeth.

If anyone is going to nervously chew through my belongings, it's going to be me.

"Calm down. It's just a pen."

"Just a pen?"

I turn to face him. He clearly wants my attention, so now he's got it.

"If that pen belonged to you, you would be free to call it anything you like. *Just* a pen. Penjamin. The little stick that magically bleeds words into your notebooks. You could chew it until it turns into paste. Drink the ink and swallow the ball at the end, if that's what your heart desires. But it isn't *just* a pen because it isn't *your* pen. It's mine, and you're chewing on it."

Somewhere between "Penjamin" and "drink the ink," I recognize that I am definitely overreacting. He's right. It really is just a pen—a very cheap one. And if I hadn't woken up this morning with a panic attack already fighting its way up my throat, I don't think I would be choking on the threat of tears right now because a boy dented its cap with his teeth.

When I graduated high school, I had the shocking realization that I'd never actually made new friends from scratch, at least not since I was a child. I've always inherited friends from other people: Boyfriends. Sport (not plural: one singular sport for one singular semester, because I thought the uniforms were cute). Orchestra. People who were forced to spend so much time with me, in such close proximity, that they eventually gave up and allowed me a temporary-ish spot on their social roster.

College would be different, especially community college. There wasn't a buzz of camaraderie or school spirit hanging in the air here. At least...not like I'd imagined there would be when compared with four-year universities.

I knew I would thrive in the kind of environment community college could offer me. I'd been looking forward to it for years.

English and Calculus 101 are the same wherever you go.

Why would I pay more for the exact same general credits?

I'd repeated these words—in my head and out loud—so many times in the last few months of my senior year that I couldn't tell who I was saying them for anymore.

I'd been desperate for a fresh start. No reminders of my past to follow me around, invading the clean slate I had waiting for me. Even so, I'd found it hard to completely ignore the small part of me that felt left out when college application season rolled around. Neither my grades nor my financial situation was doing me any favors when it came to college. I'd never planned to take the typical route of most high school seniors.

And if community college was good enough for my older brothers, it was good enough for me.

Sometimes I felt tempted to wonder if I was missing something or if I could have pushed myself harder in school. But the reality was that if I'd pushed myself any harder, I would have ended up with whatever the emotional and mental equivalent is of a hemorrhoid. One on my brain and two on my self-confidence.

Is there such a thing? Metaphorically speaking? There has to be.

I knew community college was the right move for me. I enjoyed the fresh start it provided me, in that I wouldn't know a soul on campus.

So why do I feel so lonely here?

I'd never had an issue with being lonely before. In fact, I like being alone very much, but...*oh my god.*

I think I'm lonely.

The bad kind.

The very, very bad kind.

I think I miss having friends.

I break out into a full sweat, my palms leaving wet trails on the pages of my notebook. I'm almost positive I'm not squinting, but the edges of my vision start to creep toward the center of my eyes. A dark black—so black it almost looks green—starts to cover my eyes, and I can hear my heartbeat in my ears.

My body is fully braced for the arrival of a panic attack that is already here.

I blink rapidly and focus on grabbing hold of deep breaths that feel impossible to find. Without my realizing it, my body is already operating on its own set of emergency evacuation orders.

My hands pack away my notebook.

My pencil case zips itself shut.

My water bottle slides into its home on the side of my backpack.

My feet move quickly underneath me.

My entire body is a full three steps ahead of my mind.

I'd imagine this is exactly what adrenaline was designed for, in the case of a true emergency. Unfortunately, my brain can't quite tell the difference between my life being in real danger and a guy playfully teasing me on an already Shittier Than Shitty Day.

As far as my brain is concerned, this is a life-and-death situation.

In reality: I just evacuated myself—in what must have looked like an emergency fashion—straight out of Architecture 101 and onto this bench an entire twenty-five minutes early for no reason.

If I never see another blue pen for the rest of my life, it will still be too soon. And while I'm drawing up lists of things I'd never like to see again, the same goes for guys with shaggy blond hair who smell like coffee and a freshly rolled joint.

It's a rather short list, but a definite one.

I'm trying to remember what my therapist told me to do when I have a panic attack in public. Was it to name three things I see? Three things I feel? Or...was it three things I can hear? Maybe it was all of them. I can do all of them.

I hear people laughing on another bench.
I hear the leaves rustling in the tree above me.
I hear a bird somewhere close.
I wonder if that bird has any friends.

"Are you okay?"

I see the sidewalk under my shoes.
I see a concrete tabletop stained with bird shit and old bubble gum.
My hands...I see those too.
Wow, this table is very gross.

"Hey. Are you okay?"

I see a hand waving in front of my face.
I see...No. I need to find my hands again.
I want my hands to feel like my hands again.
Oh my god, I don't think I can feel my ha—
Oh. I can feel my hands again.

"*Elyse*. Can you just tell me if you're all right?"

I raise my eyes to the familiar face in front of me. My mind is almost back in sync with my body. I try to take a deep breath through my nose, filling my lungs with fresh air. I feel my chest expand as far as it can, and I push the borrowed oxygen back out where it belongs.

I force myself to repeat this process.

Good. Do it again.

And I do.

Everything seems to be working as it should.

But surely I'm not seeing clearly...because the face that's inches away from my own is the same one I'd been staring at just a few minutes ago in class. The face that smiled at me as I realized I was lonely.

The smile that ruined my blue pen.

The blue pen I never want to see again.

"Elyse." His hands are resting on my shoulders. I'm staring up at his Adam's apple, watching it move up and down the front of his neck as he talks to me. He has a nice mouth and a very worried face.

"I know for sure I'm having a panic attack..." I say through a labored exhale. "But I also have an irrational fear of having..."

Inhale: "... both a heart attack *and* a stroke at the same time..."

Exhale: "... and unfortunately for me, the symptoms of a panic attack..."

Inhale: "... and a heart attack are too fucking similar and that's what's happening right now so please sit down *you'remakingmereallynervous*."

Exhale.

He sits down on the bench next to me and removes only one of his hands from my shoulders. I sense that he knows exactly what is happening with me. That he has experienced this many times before. I mean, it's a panic attack—doesn't everyone get them? I close my eyes and feel every nerve ending in my body shut down apart from the ones beneath his hand.

"I'm Landon. You're Elyse. We're on campus at Orange Coast College, and it's Monday morning."

I cough out a laugh and surprise myself by saying, "It's Tuesday."

"What?"

"You said it's Monday. But it's Tuesday."

"No, it isn't, it's—"

"We have Architecture together on Tuesdays and Thursdays. It's—"

"Got it. It's Tuesday." A few silent seconds pass. "So...you're feeling better then?"

I'm used to hearing his voice a few rows behind me in class, two days a week. A voice that usually sneaks in late and sneaks out early. A voice that has no name and no pens.

How does he know my *name?*

"You write your name at the top of your notebook every single time you sit down to take notes. It's the only thing you write large enough for me to see from where I sit."

I'm about 90 percent sure I asked that question silently, but my face betrays my private thoughts so frequently that I'm used to others answering my silent questions.

"You should really write everything else a little larger. It would make copying you so much easier. I attribute my C-minus to how impossibly small your handwriting is."

Deep in my stomach, I feel the urge to vomit an apology.

But once his words sink in I feel more curious than I do apologetic. Our seats are not assigned. Why doesn't he just pick a different seat and copy someone else? Someone who actually has a clue what's happening in class.

"And while we're on the topic," he continues, as if I'm playing an equal part in this very one-sided conversation, "can you settle a bet for me? Why do you write your name so large? And why do you write it on the top of every single page in your notebook? I personally think it's because you're afraid you'll forget it. I like to picture you leaving small written reminders on Post-it notes everywhere you go. Your name. Who you are. What you like. *50 First Dates* style. It's the only logical answer."

He's smiling, but his tone carries the shadow of an inside joke where I'm the punch line and I'm not allowed to know why. If I didn't know any better—and I rarely ever do—I'd think I was being teased.

Eighteen years old.

In college.

Fresh out of a panic attack.

And I feel ten all over again.

All this time spent dreaming about being in a new place, with brand-new people, has been a complete waste.

All I'd wanted was my very own Factory Reset, where I could completely unpack myself and select only the best and easiest parts of my personality to put back in. The parts people liked. The parts I created, tweaked, and fine-tuned so I would be someone that people *liked* liking. Maybe with all the strange and unlikable parts of me erased, I would transform into a Friend Maker.

And if not a Friend Maker, then, *for the love of god*, at least someone who could easily blend in.

But even *here*, I'm doing a terrible job blending in. I'm having a panic attack over a pen. My Factory Reset hasn't stuck. Is this some hellish debt I owe for being alive?

I can feel my chest getting tight again. My breathing has become so shallow that I'm barely breathing at all.

"Fuck *all the way* off."

My words emerge involuntarily. I'm as frustrated as I sound, but this near stranger doesn't deserve to know that. I sling my backpack over my shoulder while shoving his hand off. I push myself off the bench and march toward the student parking lot.

Did he *really* not get enough of a rise out of me in class? He had to follow me all the way outside for more? Wage *bets* about me in his spare time? If I hadn't already passed the window of time when you could drop a class without it showing up on your transcript, I'd drop this godforsaken class the moment I got back to my apartment tonight. This class isn't even the class I thought I was signing up for, because none of the buildings we're studying are even pretty. They all look like they were made out of shipping containers or built from a gingerbread house kit, slapped together in one business day.

I don't have a clue what's going on, and I'm running out of energy to pretend that I do.

"Shit. I'm sorry. Wait!" I hear him running after me. He's tall and catches up quickly.

"Please just leave me alone! *Please?*" I throw my voice loudly in front of me, embarrassed at how desperate I sound to get away from him. For just a moment I let myself picture how irrationally I am behaving. What I must look like to him. A batshit-crazy, second-semester community college freshman who has panic attacks over pens and cries when boys are mean.

I can't explain that I feel isolated.

That I feel stupid.

That I feel like a failure.

I can't tell him I'm exhausted from working three jobs seven days a week so I can pay my rent. That I was just ghosted by a guy who I'm positive is the only person I've ever actually fallen in love with, but he won't answer my texts unless the moon is out. I can't tell him that I've never felt like I was built to learn in a classroom.

And I definitely can't tell him those fucking pens are the only thing that makes me feel like I have an ounce of control over my brain, which likes to wander out of the room without my permission. It always has. It always will.

My teachers were right.

I wasn't made for school.

I don't belong here.

I don't realize I'm crying until a stream of snot sticks to my lips.

Perfect.

"Would you stop power walking for *two seconds*? It was a bad joke, okay? I'm sorry."

I continue to walk as fast as I can, the contents of my backpack sloshing from side to side. I narrow my eyes so I can't see his body in my peripheral vision.

Very mature, Elyse.

He is matching my pace with an incredibly insignificant amount of effort.

"I was trying to make you laugh. My timing was awful, but I was just trying to make you laugh."

I stop walking.

"Do you just sit around and make fun of me with other people? The girl who has all the pens? Who spends twenty minutes doodling her name at the top of her notes because she has no fucking clue what's happening in class but is desperate to look busy?"

"My older brother has panic attacks." His voice shoots out, and he looks even more surprised by his own vulnerability than I am. I can't help but notice that his voice had broken toward the end of his sentence.

I feel a deep line cast itself between my eyebrows, and my forehead transforms into a skin accordion as I focus on understanding—focus on putting the puzzle pieces of a person together as he stands directly in front of me—a task most people perform subconsciously, without any effort.

"He looks exactly like you did back there. He's been getting them since we were little. They used to scare me because they obviously scared the shit out of him. But I can see them coming now. The way his face looks. How he's breathing. It happens fast, but I can always tell."

Whatever version of him I'd met on the concrete bench a few minutes ago has returned, and I'm surprised by the emotion growing in my chest. It isn't panic or frustration. Is it something else? Something good?

"I still feel pretty helpless, but at least I know I can make him laugh. It's the one thing I can do. Other than that…I've got nothing. I was just trying to make you laugh. I'm sorry."

Somewhere between sixty seconds and forty minutes pass before either one of us says anything. I'm secretly hoping that a student driver will lose control and run me over before I have to come up with a response to the kindness and honesty he just offered me.

"I'm not…usually like this," I finally say. I quickly add, "That's actually a lie. I'm pretty much like this all the time."

"I think you're just fine."

His tone is flat and even. I wait for the rest of the joke, but it never comes. He really is trying to be kind. I typically wouldn't consider being called "just fine" a compliment, but given the circumstances, I catch myself blushing at his response. I don't feel like I deserve an ounce of kindness from this person, but here he is, offering it.

"I wouldn't consider myself 'fine' in any sense of the word. But either way, that's for me and a therapist to figure out. I'll be fine one day, probably."

"If you have any recommendations for good therapists, let me know. I left mine back in Colorado and I haven't been able to find one since. I did actually try the free counseling sessions they offer here on campus. When I walked into my first session, the therapist waiting to meet with me was someone I dated for a few weeks when I first enrolled here. That was...that was a lot."

No fewer than ten questions pop into my head, all at once. I have no clue how to prioritize them. They all feel equally urgent.

"Colorado!" I say, with absolutely no hint of a question in my voice. I'm so focused on making sure I don't lead with the whole dating-the-therapist thing that my mouth doesn't wait for my brain to turn the thought into a question.

My post–panic attack conversation skills are about as smooth as sandpaper.

"Colorado," he offers plainly in return. He shoves both hands into the pockets of his brown corduroy pants.

"Colorado. Very cool. I mean...I've never actually been. But it *sounds* very cool. Mountains, snow, other...Denver things." My hands gesture toward the sky, and I'm very aware of how little I actually care to know about Colorado. Especially when the alternative is asking for more details about the time he walked into a free therapy session and was surprised to find a person he'd probably kissed on the mouth. I can google facts about Colorado. He is the only person who could tell me about the therapist.

"I can tell by the way you're looking directly *through* me that you have more questions. I'd be happy to answer them, but before that, I'm going to need some breakfast."

I look at the watch that has lived reliably on my left wrist for so long that the anatomy of my arm underneath has started to make room for it. The groove in my wrist is proof that I'm a complete stranger to change. The Factory Reset never stood a chance.

"Oh my god, it's already ten fifteen! I have to get to my next class in a few minutes."

"Do you like breakfast burritos?"

Wait, what?

"Well, I do. But I got carsick after eating a breakfast burrito once as a kid, and I haven't been able to eat one since—" I stop myself from continuing.

New people.

New place.

I can be somebody who eats spontaneous breakfast burritos.

"Mm-hmm, I like breakfast burritos. A breakfast burrito sounds really good."

It absolutely does not, but it *does* sound better than sitting through English 101.

"You're gonna like this place. Promise." He walks confidently ahead of me toward the student lot, adding, "You're driving! I'm way too high!"

"But...didn't...you drive here?"

"There's this magical thing called 'hot boxing,' Elyse. You should try it sometime. I think you'd really enjoy it!" He's still walking forward.

I jog to catch up to him so I can lead him to Gloria, the Toyota RAV4 my mom sold to me when I graduated high school.

Everything about my car is perfect, besides the paw-print license plate frame my mom had installed when Gloria was hers.

"FUN!" he says mockingly, while gently kicking my bumper to bring attention to the black-and-white paw prints dancing around my license plate.

"Those came with the car," I say defensively.

"I figured," he says through a smile.

I sit in the driver's seat with my seat belt buckled over my chest and waist and my hands gripping the steering wheel as I wait to start the car. I realize I'm in my car with a near stranger.

"My name is Elyse, by the way. I mean, I know you already knew that. But until ten minutes ago, I didn't *know* you already knew that. It just feels weird driving away from campus with you in my car before actually introducing myself. So your...name is Landon? Right?"

"Right. Landon. Nice to officially meet you."

We shake hands, which feels way too formal considering the events that have taken place in the last thirty minutes. Either way, I shake his hand with far too much force.

I'm positive I overdid it.

Neither of us seems surprised.

Landon calls out turn-by-turn directions to one of his favorite breakfast burrito spots five minutes from campus. I hadn't realized how hungry I was until we walked in. I copy his order exactly.

There isn't anything particularly fancy about this place—just an average-size room with loose tables and chairs bumping into each other as if they were thrown around in the wake of hungry customers. But somehow it feels like an extension of someone's living room. I like that very much.

I'm flooded with memories of my grandpa John's tamale-making parties and the jobs he would assign to people before they even had a chance to sit down. Grandpa John loved food with his whole heart, and he loved people even more, so a day centered around food *and* people was practically Heaven on Earth for him. I liked his tamale-making parties too, but for different reasons. Mainly because I felt special when Grandpa John would sneak me small taste tests of the ingredients he was working with and ask me to "make sure nothing was poisoned."

While Landon and I wait for our food, I'm already taking mental notes to come back to this restaurant again. Maybe alone, so I can enjoy the full experience without the added pressure of conversation and getting the ratio of eye-contact-to-no-eye-contact *juuussstttt* right.

Our order numbers are shouted from behind the counter at a volume that I assume is meant to reach the farthest corners of the patio outside.

I jump...aggressively.

"Sorry, mija!" The source of the booming voice is a woman at least six inches shorter than me, wearing white plastic gloves that I can only imagine make the heat in the kitchen feel that much more suffocating. Her voice is much softer now.

"Oh my gosh, no, you're fine. I'm just jumpy. Sorry. And thank you! *Sorry.*" I grab the tray holding a child-size burrito wrapped in yellow paper.

And by child-size, I mean *exactly* that.

The size of a small child.

Possibly the largest burrito I've ever seen in my life.

Landon scans the seating area without much purpose, as if he already knows where he wants to sit. He turns around, walks straight out the front door, and sits on the second bench from the entrance, just close enough to still feel a part of the kitchen's energy, but far enough away to be released from the hot burrito air coming from the kitchen. I let out a sigh of gratitude, because the heat had made me want to crawl out of my skin. Eating when I feel hot is nearly impossible, but I won't tell Landon that.

"I would sell my soul to be able to make breakfast burritos that taste as good as these," Landon says as he rips open the intricate wrapping. He pays absolutely no attention to the way the burrito is wrapped or the fact that there is a *correct* way to unwrap it while keeping some of the paper intact to shield his hands from touching the contents of the burrito as they fall out.

But that's fine.

As I unwrap my breakfast burrito the correct way, Landon's enthusiastic chewing is replaced with silence. He looks at my hands, which are working as methodically as they typically do.

"Are you always so...specific?"

"That might be the nicest and most roundabout way someone's ever asked me if I have OCD. But yes, I am always this *specific*, unfortunately. Clinically diagnosed as obsessively specific." I raise my burrito a few inches into the air as a silent submission of proof. "Except for when it comes to my personal space, which always surprises people. I've had a pile of clothes living on the side of my bed for a few weeks now, which only gets larger by the day. It looks messy, but I could tell you every single article of clothing in that pile right now, if you asked me to. If I can't see something, my brain forgets it exists. So...everything eventually ends up in piles."

"I can respect that." He nods into his burrito and returns to eating with renewed excitement. An unspoken agreement settles between us as we eat our burritos: We'll pick our conversation back up when we're done eating.

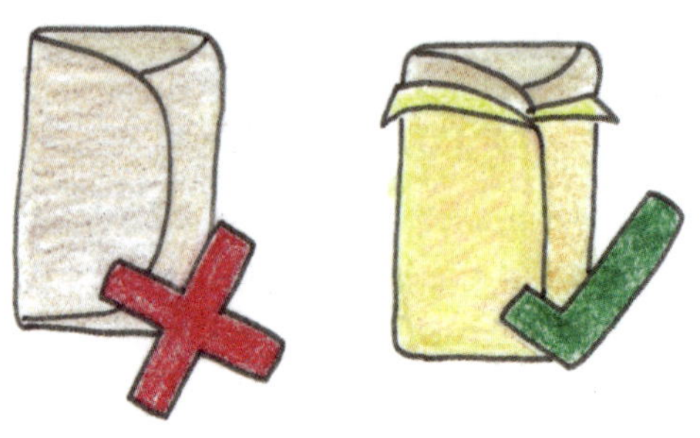

1

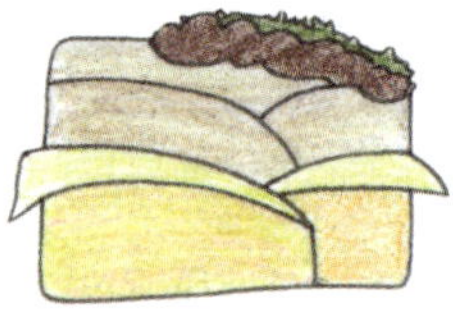

2

3

4

It's nice to take bite after bite without the possibility of a question looming over me. I break my silence only after Landon lightly chokes on a bite that's a little too big. Between the coughs, he stares at the burrito as if it's betrayed him.

"If I'm going to die, this isn't the worst way to go out." He isn't all the way done coughing but is already taking another bite—somehow one that's even larger than the bite that made him choke.

"So...are we just *not* going to talk about the whole therapist girlfriend situation? Because I was promised answers after breakfast." I gesture toward the only food that remains on his lap: a few chunks of chorizo-stained potato and melted cheese that cling to the wrapper.

"Grace. Oh my god, Grace. I could have died right there in the doorway when I walked into her practice office..."

We are sitting side by side on the bench as he tells me the story. For most of the conversation, we look straight ahead. I'm not distracted by the burden of getting the eye-contact-to-no-eye-contact ratio perfectly right, which makes his story even more captivating than it already is.

They'd met at a house party his brother threw in their shared apartment.

A friend of a friend of a friend.

She was a grad student who occasionally earned training hours on campus.

He didn't know that.

He asked her out to coffee the next day.

They slept together the day after that.

From there, they met only a few more times.

Usually late at night. Usually for the same thing.

They both wanted something casual, which is exactly what they were.

He mentioned that he was still looking for a therapist.

She suggested he take advantage of the free resources the school provided.

When he walked into his first session, *she* was his student therapist.

He thought briefly about sitting down on the couch across from her, but he walked out instead.

To this day he still has absolutely no clue if it was just a coincidence or the result of her handiwork.

"Holy..." My voice trails off. I *really* don't want to make any assumptions.

"I know. I'm sure you came to the same conclusion I did that day. But I'm going to chalk it up to a coincidence so I'm not constantly haunted by the memory...or looking over my shoulder to see if she's there."

"I was going to ask if you saw the girl in that parked car holding the giant binoculars, but..." I point at a parked car across the street but laugh before I can finish the rest of my sentence. His laugh eventually joins mine, and for a brief moment I forget how horribly the day started, how heavy my chest felt when I woke up. I feel so happy right now. I don't feel lonely or "specific" or anxious.

Just...happy.

He's so nice, and I feel happy and happy feels *nice*.

As quickly as the relief of forgetting washes over me, panic replaces it.

Oh my god, what if he thinks this is a date?

I'm not entirely sure where the thought came from, but here it is.

"This isn't a date," I say, a few notches louder and faster than I meant to.

Landon is still mid-laugh as the statement jolts out of my mouth. I'd clearly surprised both of us with the urgency of those four words. I watch as his face quickly passes through a range of different emotions, starting at amused and ending somewhere near confused.

"Sorry...?" He waits for me to explain.

I angle my body slightly toward him from the other end of the bench. Just barely, but not enough to maintain eye contact if I start to feel more embarrassed than I already am.

"This." I point back and forth between the two of us a few times, my wrist looking completely boneless. "*This* isn't a date. It can't be a date. I don't want it to be. I...needed to make sure you knew that. And that I knew that. And that *you* knew that *I* knew that. It's just that I...have a unique skill of ending up on dates without knowing it. People can be so vague, you know? I just wanted to confirm that breakfast burritos are *only* breakfast burritos and that this *isn't* a date. Because I really don't want this to be a date."

Why don't you just punch him in the face while you're at it?

He gets it.

Stop talking.

"Um..." His expression is nearly unreadable now. If I had to guess, I might say pity is what I'm seeing?

Oh god, please don't be pity.

"I don't want you to take this the wrong way, but...*in no way* did I think this was a date. I just wanted to make sure that you knew I wasn't a complete asshole after how I acted in class today. And the classes before today. And then again outside. Wait, am I just an asshole?"

"It's definitely possible!" My tone is reassuring. My words are not.

"Anyway...no, I didn't think this was a date. I thought *maybe* I'd be able to make a new friend. But mostly I was just focused on fixing the me-being-an-asshole thing. I didn't even consider the thought that this might seem like a date..."

Did he just...does he want to...did he say "friend"?

Does he want me to be his friend?

...Am I a Friend Maker?

"It's so *fucking hard* to make friends at this school." Landon stops and waits a few moments before continuing. "*Especially* with students who are a full fifteen years older than me. My brother, Michael, is so good at making friends. I joke that he's the 'People Collector,' and somehow, the gene skipped right over me. I'm lucky that I inherit his friendships, but that doesn't mean I feel particularly close to those people. It feels pretty awful, to be honest. It's like...those friendships require a secret ingredient *only* Michael can add. When he's not there, they simply don't work."

If I could have any superpower, it would be the ability to project my feelings, thoughts, and memories onto a wall so others could fully understand me without the obstacle of me failing to explain things to them. The superpower would be perfect for exactly this moment. I sit there feeling stuck, wishing I could explain to Landon how deeply I understand every single word he just shared.

I'm sure that if I open my mouth to speak, I'll be interrupted by my own tears.

I'm happy to feel so immediately known by a stranger, but I wish we could relate to each other in a different way. A way that didn't make us feel so lonely. I wish this for Landon *and* for myself.

I can feel the heaviness of his words sinking into him from across the bench. "If it makes you feel any better, I don't think I've ever been good at it. The whole...friend thing."

I need to say more, but my throat is on fire. I owe him more, for how much honesty he's offered me today.

Just keep going, Elyse. You can say more.

"Have you ever been stuck in one of those nightmares where you try screaming and nothing comes out? It's like I'm living the real-life version of that every time I get close enough to someone to consider them a friend. I feel like I trick them by being able to talk while they're still a stranger. And then one day, I'm...I'm screaming and nothing is coming out. Sometimes I feel scared to let people become a permanent part of my life because then, if or when they decide to leave, I'll be forced to miss them. And I've been forced to miss a lot of people. I'm really tired of missing people. So it's easier to just...not."

The tears start falling from my eyes and down my cheeks about three syllables into the "more" I decided to confess. Landon allows me the illusion of privacy as we both look straight ahead. Maybe that's why I don't feel like I'm oversharing, as I often do.

"I'm sorry," he offers, only after he's sure that I've finished my thought completely.

"It's all right." I drag my forearm across my face, cleaning the snot from my nose before it spills out any further. With it, I remove a few pieces of melted cheese that were apparently stuck somewhere near my mouth.

"That's what therapy is for, *amiritttttte*?"

I laugh through one final sob.

Snot shoots out of my nose.

I would dare to feel embarrassed, but instead I'm secretly grateful that my snot rocket lightened the mood. The air around us instantly feels a hundred times lighter, but the truth we've shared with each other still remains in reach, close enough for us to grab ahold of again if we want to.

I look at my watch. It's almost noon.

"Well..." I stand in front of the bench, passing my keys back and forth between my hands. He slaps his hands together just once and gets off the bench to stand next to me. "I need to get to work. Can I take you back to campus?"

The first three minutes of our drive back to Landon's car are spent in a comfortable silence.

The last two are filled with some of the most awful music I've ever heard in my life. I have never more thoroughly regretted handing someone an aux cord.

"SO YOU'RE TELLING ME YOU'VE NEVER HEARD OF *SKA PUNK* BEFORE??" Landon screams over the noise that he apparently classifies as music.

"THIS HAS A *NAME*?!" I yell back, doing my best to sound fun and not at all overstimulated at the competing instruments and tempos bleeding out of my car's speakers.

I'm not sure what the threshold is for decibels of sound the human eardrum can safely tolerate. But whatever that number is? We passed it a few streets ago. I think if I'm forced to listen to this any longer I won't be safe to drive. I pull into the same parking spot that I had this morning.

"I just realized I have no idea what your car—"

"WHAT?" Landon cuts me off before I'm finished.

"I SAID I JUST REALIZED...I HAVE NO IDEA...WHAT YOUR *CAR* LOOKS LIKE!"

Landon is playfully pointing to his ears to signal that he still can't understand me. I stop yelling over the music and yank the aux cord out of its port. I could have just turned the volume all the way down, but that wouldn't feel nearly satisfying enough, given the level of panic this music has been causing me.

The sound stops abruptly, but not before a terrifying electric crackle and *POP!* punctuates the already overwhelming last couple of minutes.

My ears are ringing, and I take a deep breath. *"I don't know where you parked."* My words are no longer underlined with Ear-Bleeding Music.

He is already halfway out of my car. "Why didn't you just say that?"

My ears are still ringing.

I wonder what would happen to me if the ringing never stopped.

Is that possible?

That's a suffocating thought.

"Hey, I meant it, by the way!"

"Meant...what?" I yell back through the glass of my car window. It takes its sweet time rolling down. I've never paid attention to the speed of my automatic windows until today.

They are painfully slow.

"The friend thing. There's no pressure, obviously. But I meant what I said back there. It would be kinda nice to have a friend here."

"Yeah, I agree. Having a friend here would be really nice." My words feel more like a confession than a response.

"That settles it then. We're friends!"

"Friends." I mime a handshake but realize it's actually quite awkward to mime only one side of a handshake. My other hand steps in to play the role of Landon's Hand, so I look like I'm holding my own hand and moving it up and down. I don't think this gesture is conveying what I want it to.

"Anyway...I'm gonna go sit in my car and take a nap." He waves and walks deeper into the student lot. I start driving to work.

"See you Thursday," I say to myself.

I see the car driving in front of me.

I hear the air conditioner blowing loudly out the vents.

I feel happy.

I think I just made a friend.

THE ELEVATOR TO

PARIS

There's Been a Misunderstanding

We walk into the nightclub and I grab a seat at the bar. My friends go and make new friends on the dance floor. My brain is still getting accustomed to a legal drinking age that's three years younger than it is back home. I'm still shocked to see an eighteen-year-old confidently drinking alcohol in public without looking over their shoulder or chugging it in the girls' restroom out of a crinkled-up water bottle.

Unfortunately, I have not had a personality transplant since leaving my dorm and immediately regret coming out for the night.

My drink is gone before I can even register what I'm tasting. Though I want another, I'd brought only enough cash with me for one drink. It's probably for the best. In an effort to save money this evening, we'd all enjoyed a *very* festive pregame back in our dorm before going out for the night. I can already feel Tomorrow Elyse cursing Tonight Elyse while I sit here in this spinning room.

I close my tab with the bartender and wonder how safe it would be if I left the nightclub and walked home by myself. As I set a handful of two-euro coins onto my bill, I see a man in a white button-up, which is *definitely* one size too small, walking toward me. I assume it isn't an accident that the top three buttons of his shirt are unfastened, exposing the suspiciously hairless skin on his chest. He is beautiful—not in a way that immediately makes me swoon, but in the way a painting is beautiful. Before I can think, I spin 180 degrees in my seat to face the bartender again. I'd felt my face flush as I watched White Button-Up walk across the room, and I want to hide my crimson cheeks.

Every single person I've met while living in Paris has reminded me of someone I know back home...just the hotter and more relaxed version.

(Who also smoke cigarettes whenever they drink.)

Is it their style?

How comfortable they seem in their skin?

Or are they really just *that much* more attractive?

Standing in front of Parisians makes me wish I had one of those Tiny Museum Headsets. You know, the ones that you rent at the help desk that come with audiotapes and a free side of shame? Those headsets always make me feel like I need help catching up on the culture and context I clearly lack in order to fully appreciate the beauty of the art in front of me.

I wish I had one of *those* to fully appreciate Parisians.

They are living art.

I begin imagining how grateful I would be if I had a Tiny Museum Headset for *every* situation in life. Can't read social cues? Tiny headset. Can't remember if your best friend is currently on again or off again with her not-boyfriend? Tiny headset!

"What's so funny?"

A voice snaps me out of whatever Tiny Museum Headset trance I accidentally put myself in, and I shake my head to return to reality. White Button-Up is now sitting on the barstool beside me.

Whatever I'd planned to say suddenly doesn't seem good enough. Unfortunately, I have no backup to *Oh, nothing! I'm just thinking about museum headsets!* Instead, I sit in complete silence.

Now would be a good time to say something, Elyse.

Literally anything.

I am staring at White Button-Up and nothing is coming out of my mouth.

As my brain continues to buffer, I realize I am eye level with his exposed chest. "Tiny museum headsets," I finally manage to say.

"Excusez-moi?" He's confused. I'm embarrassed.

"It's not...never mind. Sorry." I turn into myself, with my head down and my hands around my empty glass. I think my default factory setting is Apologetic. Especially when I have no reason to be. I panic, because my knowledge of the French language, at this point, is conversational at best. And by "at best" I mean when I'm sober. I can feel my mind going much slower after a couple of drinks. If White Button-Up plans on having a conversation with me beyond "Good morning," "Good evening," "Good night," and "Where is the bathroom?" then unfortunately we're going to have a very short conversation.

Record-breakingly short.

"You want company tonight?"

I think he's talking to...me? He *is* talking to me, right? I look behind and beside me to ensure I don't make myself look even more dense than I already look. I must have been silent longer than I thought, because he adds a follow-up:

"Don't worry, I am cheap."

Great. I've made the man beg just to sit down. I'm off to a fantastic start.

"I mean...I won't say no!"

What kind of answer is that?!

"Uh—I mean, yes, sure. That would be great. My friends are around here somewhere. I didn't come here alone. I mean, I am here *alone*, as in not in a pair. Not in a couple. I'm trying to say

I'm single. But I came here with people, so I'm not *alone* alone..."

I continue to fill the air with words that are loosely related to one another, hoping he'll cut me off and put me out of my misery. He's a gentleman, unfortunately. I continue.

"Being alone isn't a bad thing. In fact, it's kind of nice. Boyfriends are nice too, but so is being alone. I'm not a *loner* or anything. I'm just introverted. Are you introverted or extroverted?"

My brain is in outer space, and my mouth is on autopilot.

I would like to disappear.

"You want to be alone, no? I can leave?"

"No no no no no no no *no*. No, that's not—you can stay! Eh, rester...? Rester, yes? Stay!"

This is not going well.

We spend the next ten minutes attempting to make small talk through our language barrier. I have never wished I paid attention in class *more* than right now. After a few questions are asked and answered, I meet the eye of one of my friends dancing across the club. Stella is clearly waiting for me to give a glance so she can start preparing her next steps if interference is needed.

There are three universal glances you must know and have ready to go at any moment.

The Glances: A Comprehensive Breakdown

 **GLANCE NO. 1: VERY BAD**

WHAT IT MEANS: I'm not safe. I'm uncomfortable. I need you to save me.

DESIRED OUTCOME: The friend on the receiving end of this glance interrupts the conversation you are in and saves you from an uncomfortable romantic or social interaction.

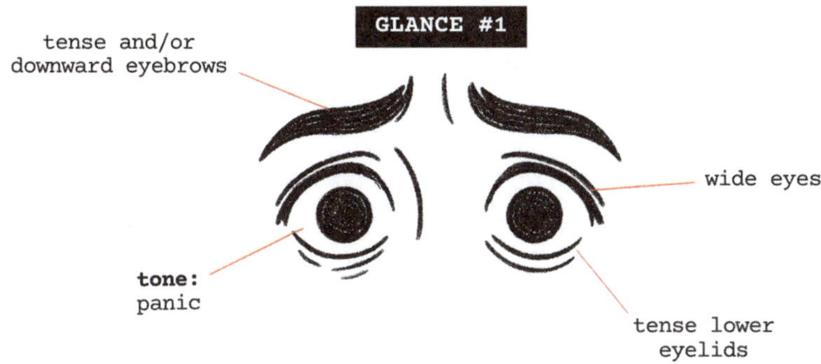
GLANCE #1
tense and/or downward eyebrows
wide eyes
tone: panic
tense lower eyelids

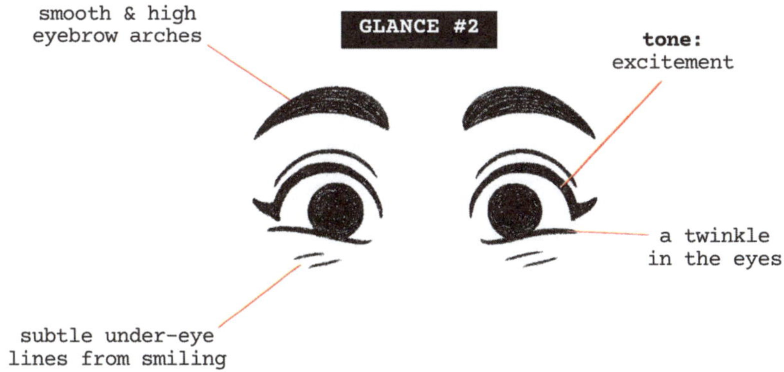
smooth & high eyebrow arches
GLANCE #2
tone: excitement
a twinkle in the eyes
subtle under-eye lines from smiling

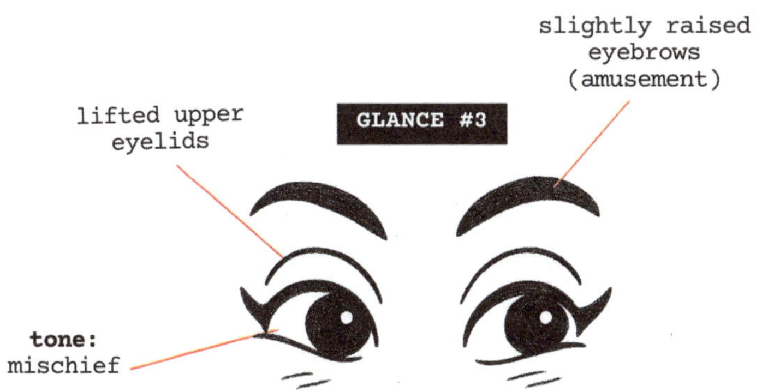
slightly raised eyebrows (amusement)
lifted upper eyelids
GLANCE #3
tone: mischief

GLANCE NO. 2: VERY GOOD

WHAT IT MEANS: I'm safe. I'm enjoying myself. I want it to lead to more!

DESIRED OUTCOME: The friend receiving the glance stays a respectful distance away, ready to body-slam anyone who tries to interrupt your conversation.

GLANCE NO. 3: BOTH VERY GOOD & VERY BAD

WHAT IT MEANS: I'm safe. I'm in the middle of hearing or experiencing something that we are definitely going to be debriefing later. GET READY!!

DESIRED OUTCOME: The friend receiving the glance keeps a respectful distance from your conversation, but the moment you're alone together, they remind you to share every detail you can possibly remember from that conversation.

No interference needed. I quickly give Stella Glance No. 2, hoping she's able to see the subtle reassurance I'm sending with my eyeballs, given that this room seems like it's lit by one single light bulb. I continue my sad attempt at flirting in a language I am actively studying—and failing—in school. White Button-Up refreshes my vodka tonic alongside his glass of red wine. This is turning out to be one of the more successful encounters I've ever had with the opposite sex.

And it only took flying more than five thousand miles away from home and draining my entire life savings.

I'll take it.

Out of the corner of my eye I can see my classmates huddling in a circle near the exit of the club. I turned toward the bartender to close out my tab and remember that I don't have any more cash with me.

"Close out?" the bartender asks.

I wish it wasn't so obvious that I'm American.

"Oui, merci," I say in my best accent.

I take my bill from the bartender, but White Button-Up kindly grabs it from me with one hand and places his other hand on his chest.

"Me," he says with a smile.

I am equal parts blinded by his incredible smile and grateful he offered to pay for my drink. This man is more attractive than the actors they cast in perfume commercials. What is he doing standing next to me? The only logical conclusion I can piece together is that I've fallen on my way to the bathroom, have hit my head, and am hallucinating. This doesn't just *happen*.

This is another moment when a Tiny Museum Headset would be useful. I'd like it to explain to me what the hell is happening right now.

"Unless you don't want me to pay?"

"Oh my god, no…I'm sorry. No, yes, that's fine. Thank you. Sorry."

White Button-Up laughs. "No or yes?"

"Sorry. Yes."

"You say sorry too much."

"I know. I'm—" It's taking an enormous amount of restraint not to apologize again. This time, for apologizing.

White Button-Up leaves enough cash to pay for both our bills and stands next to me as I gather my things. I'm not entirely sure where my group is going next, but I assume it will have something to do with food; we've been drinking since class got out at three in the afternoon, and the clock is now inching close to midnight. I shuffle through what I've eaten today: a chicken and cheese panini this morning at ten, a coffee at two, the bottle of wine I shared with my roommate Stella, and a pain au chocolat I took two bites of and then forgot existed as soon as Stella and I started taking Going-Out Pictures before leaving. My stomach is churning thinking about how many hours I've been drinking without a proper meal.

By the looks of it we've picked up a few other new additions to our cohort this evening. With just enough liquid courage, I turn to White Button-Up and ask if he wants to join my group for the rest of the evening. He agrees and slowly introduces himself to everyone standing in the huddle.

Stella is showing off her A-plus French skills to White Button-Up as I'm negotiating with the others on where we should pick up food before walking back to our dorm. I campaign for the falafel cart I've become obsessed with since living here, mostly because someone told me on my first day of school that it was Lenny Kravitz's favorite falafel place in Paris. I've never bothered to look this up. I am more than happy to accept this as a fact and make it *my* favorite falafel place in Paris. My favorite, and also my first. I was too embarrassed to ask, *What the hell is a falafel?*

I look up the name and address of Lenny's and my favorite falafel stand to see if it is anywhere near the club we are in, and Google tells me it is already closed. We settle on a spot a few doors down that sells pizza by the slice.

I wonder if Lenny Kravitz has a favorite pizza spot in Paris too...

Our group remains close together through the back alleys and cobblestone sidewalks of the Latin Quarter. We are in one of the oldest districts in Paris, surrounded by beautiful and historic landmarks. But all I can think about is the fact that I just suggested pizza and I don't have enough money to pay for a slice of pizza.

I move myself to the back of the line as everyone else frantically presses themselves against the thin glass window at the front of the shop. Pizza can't solve every problem, but it can definitely solve our group's most urgent problem this evening: sour stomachs.

Stella knows I can't spontaneously pay for food I didn't budget for, so I do my best to hide from her eyeline. I don't enjoy talking about money with her, simply because I don't have much of it and she does. Knowing that, she is *never* shy about making sure I have what I need and sometimes even what I want. I frequently protest her generosity, but she never relents.

Of all the strangers I could have been randomly assigned as a roommate, I'm so grateful it was Stella. But tonight of all nights, I really don't want to have a loud conversation about finances that ends with her buying me a piece of margherita pizza.

Especially in front of White Button-Up.

I can't think of many things more humiliating.

I feel my only option is to squat down on the cobblestone sidewalk at the back of the line and hope that Stella doesn't notice me before she gets pulled in by the Pizza Man's shouting.

"Are you...okay?" White Button-Up asks from way up there.

I hadn't thought twice about sitting directly onto the cold ground, nor the possibility that I'd look like a crazy person to this stranger. If I explain that I'm hiding from Stella because I don't have enough money to buy myself an emergency slice of pizza, then I'll embarrass myself. But if I *don't* explain why I suddenly dropped down to the ground like I'm on fire and had to Stop, Drop, and Roll, then I'll *also* embarrass myself.

Either way you slice this pizza, I lose.

My least favorite kind of pizza is a lose-lose pizza.

I open my mouth and hope for the best.

"Oh, I'm fine! I'm incredible, actually! I just suddenly realized my feet were sore, so I sat down. On the ground."

I gently touch the sidewalk with my hand, the same way someone would pat the empty seat next to them on a couch as an invitation to sit next to them.

I don't see the empty bench next to me until White Button-Up responds by saying nothing at all and looking directly at it. The bench is close enough for me to reach out and touch it.

"So you want pizza, yes?"

I purse my lips, wave my hands, and shake my head as if the mere thought of pizza disgusts me.

"This was your idea, and you do not want it?"

"You're right. Yes. But I don't really want it. I mean, I *want* it, I just don't want it right now...like...ummmmm, I mean...what *do* I mean?"

The longer I drag this sentence out, the less familiar my voice sounds to me. I actually start to transition into a voice that I believe my subconscious brain reserves only for special moments like this one. Moments I can only describe as a unique type of hell designed specifically for me and me alone.

I'm really struggling to tell him I can't afford this pizza.

"I can't pay for it..."

There. That wasn't so difficult, was it?

"You can pay me back in the room."

It's fine. This is fine. Everything is going to be fine.

With our slices of pizza folded in our hands, my classmates and I walk back toward our dorm with our new friends, discussing what the rest of the night holds for us. As we walk, White Button-Up and I fall behind a few paces from the rest of the group. As much as I want to rely on the charm of my more extroverted classmates, I know at some point I have to maintain a one-on-one conversation with White Button-Up if I have any chance at seeing this man again.

I have enough friends, and by "enough" I mean, like, two, because that's about as many friendships as I can realistically maintain at any given time. Any more than that and I start to forget people exist when they're not directly in front of me. I'm more interested in figuring out if the universe is pranking me by sending me this gorgeous specimen of a man or if he's actually sticking by my side tonight because he's attracted to me.

I'm watching my classmates in front of me talk to one another with ease. I wonder what it feels like to be so comfortable around other people that the loudest sound you hear is the other person talking to you. For as long as I can remember, I've heard no fewer than seventeen competing conversations in my head before I can answer the questions I'm being asked by other people.

I overhear something about board games and beer coming from the front of the group, which is more of a relief than it should be. From the moment I walked out of the nightclub with White Button-Up, I've been scouring every dusty corner of my brain to come up with group activities that would keep everyone awake and together in one room.

Apparently my game plan is to group-hangout my way into spending more time with White Button-Up. It's been said that you're only as interesting as the company you keep.

By that logic alone, I feel like my plan has some serious potential.

Oh my god, is *this* a date?

Hold on. Just one thing at a time.

"S-so...do you like pizza?"

This is the first sentence that's left my mouth in at least two blocks, and it comes out as a whisper. My throat is so dry I feel like I swallowed dust. What kind of question is that? Who doesn't like pizza? He just ate pizza, didn't he? I'm supposed to be channeling my easy, breezy, beautiful French CoverGirl.

But right now, all I'm channeling is a panic attack.

"Of course. But American pizza is very different to pizza here, no?" He seems genuinely interested in my thoughts on this comparison, which somehow makes me even more nervous. His undivided attention feels like too much attention.

"Different. Completely different! There's no possible way that Domino's"—I point to my left—"and the slice of magic I just ate"—now pointing to my right—"could be classified as the same food. They're both delicious, but not the same *at all*."

He presses his lips together and the corner of his mouth smiles. He seems pleased by my comparison, which makes me feel like I answered the question correctly. Relief floods my body, and for the first time the entire evening, I feel comfortable standing next to this gorgeous stranger. I don't realize I've lost all feeling in my fingertips until I release my hands from the death grip they have around absolutely nothing but the outside air. I can feel blood start to sweep through the sandy pins and needles that were in my fingertips a moment ago.

I shake my hands to speed up the process.

My limbs start receiving the appropriate amount of blood flow.

My nerves settle.

I think this is going well!

"I could say the same thing about American and Parisian men!"

"...I am pizza?" White Button-Up laughs.

"No, no, that's—that's not what I mean. You know what I mean. Maybe you don't know what I mean. What I'm *trying to say* is...you're very different from the guys—umm, men—I've talked to before."

"How do you mean?"

"I mean, look at you! There are buttons on your shirt! That makes you more of an adult than anyone I've ever talked to. But then...*look at you*. You are so beautiful. I don't know how else to describe you. Handsome isn't quite nearly enough. You go to nightclubs by yourself. You're comfortable ordering a drink alone. You ask questions. Your eye contact is a holy experience. So holy that I'm almost afraid to look directly into your eyes right now. In a good way."

What was once a mere snowball of an idea to compliment this man has turned into a Word Vomit Avalanche, and I can't stop it.

My mouth officially feels out of my control.

"That's it?" I think this is sarcasm from White Button-Up. I think he's making a joke, and I think I like him very much.

I think I'm drunk.

"That's not even close to being all. You smell like a wild garden of flowers in the middle of a pine tree forest. When you ate your pizza, you looked like a walking advertisement for pizza. I wanted to buy *more pizza* simply because of the way you ate your pizza. Pizza is not an objectively sexy food, but you've made it one. And look at your hair. It's perfectly placed, like a Ken doll. Have you ever seen a Ken doll? You probably haven't. Here, I'll show you. This is what a Ken doll looks li—"

He intercepts my attempt at a mid-conversation Google search by placing his hand over my phone as I take it out of my pocket. His hand rests on top of mine in the process. It is so warm. Unbelievably warm. Like maybe the warmest hand I've ever touched in my life. I put my other hand on top of his.

"It's impressive that your hands aren't sweaty."

That's...not what I wanted to say at all?

"I'm sorry?" he asks.

"Your hands. They're warm without being sweaty. That's impressive. My hands sweat all the time. I don't even need to be warm for them to sweat. That's why I usually avoid holding hands with people. I don't want them to feel how sweaty my hands are."

I don't know why I'm saying any of this out loud. Before I can change the topic, White Button-Up grabs my hand and gently places it in his.

If I had one hundred guesses for what I thought tonight would look like, I wouldn't have come *close* to guessing this.

This...I was not ready for *this*.

The warmth from his hand is so loud that everything else in my brain feels quiet. My thoughts are at a complete halt. My inner voice isn't competing with itself for my attention. Nothing can compete with the way it feels for my hand to be held like this.

Unprompted, and because he wants to.

If this is what happens when you get out of your house, then I really need to get out more often.

"Thank you," I say.

I'm not familiar with proper Hand-Holding Etiquette. Am I even supposed to be thanking him? I hope he doesn't think I want him to stop.

Oh god, please don't stop holding my hand.

"That was a 'Thank You For Holding My Hand Please Don't Stop' kind of 'Thank You.' Just in case you were wondering. Not that you were wondering. But just in case you were."

By now, every member of my cohort has noticed us holding hands in the back of the single-file line we've fallen into as we all walk together. I can hear people in the front whispering about us. Stella frantically meets my eye to telepathically check in with me and ensure I still want the company of this handsome stranger. The look on her face is a mixture of concern and surprise as she receives Glance No. 2 from me.

I don't think anyone is as surprised at my social success tonight as I am.

Well, maybe anyone besides myself *and* Stella. Having shared a room with me for three months, she is painfully aware of how unprecedented the happenings of tonight have been.

Stella gives me a reassuring smile, then returns to her conversation in the front. I'd like nothing more than to interpret it as a silent vote of confidence, even though a part of my brain is doing everything in its power to convince me—in some deeply subconscious way—that her smile is her special way of mocking me rather than encouraging me.

I wonder if she's mad at me.

She's probably not mad at me.

She might be.

She isn't.

Is she?

I would really like a Tiny Museum Headset.

I'm not sure if it's the way the air smells, the buzz of my drinks hitting my bloodstream, or the feeling of being admired by someone well out of my league...but I feel like I am levitating down the streets of Paris.

I'm not sure how long I've been silent. The silence doesn't bother me like it usually does. On a normal day, I tend to fill each waking moment with sound in hopes that I don't lose the interest of those around me. I'm scared to be still and quiet because that might allow others the opportunity to realize they don't actually want to be around me. If I keep conversation moving forward, if I keep asking questions, if I fill every silent space, if I keep talking...then people won't have time to become bored of me the way I assume they inevitably will.

But this isn't a normal day. This is a Very Not Normal Day.

After walking for over an hour, we are now in sight of our university. I can see the gorgeous buildings peering over the shops that surround it. I've never seen buildings quite like the ones that exist in Paris. Up until now, I've never thought much of architecture, if at all. But it's hard to ignore the beauty of even the simplest buildings here. If the architecture class I took last semester would have covered buildings like the ones I'm staring at right now, I think I would have paid better attention.

As beautiful as the dorm building is, I'm disappointed to be standing in front of it. I wish I could hold back time and keep tonight from slipping away from me. I can hear the sound of the crosswalk beeping in the distance, and for the first time in an hour, my entire group has reassembled. Stella is close enough to touch, and I am silently begging for her to take her Most Stella Form and begin loudly organizing plans for the group the way she typically does.

"Before we get to where you sleep...when would you like to pay?"

"Oh, I'm so sorry. I thought I already mentioned it earlier. I don't have any cash left in my wallet. I spent it all back at the bar. But I do have cash in my room! It's just...I didn't expect to be out this late."

"When we go to your room, you can pay me there."

Chivalry is not dead. But it does feel like it's on life support at the moment.

I can feel my face turning red. Am I crazy, or did we already discuss that I'd be paying him back for that slice of pizza when I got back to my dorm?

"That's a great plan. Again, thank you for the pizza. And also, I'm sorry."

"Sorry for what?"

"Well, a lot of things. All the time. But right now, for the pizza. I don't want you to think I intentionally suggested ordering food I couldn't pay for. I don't usually accept things for free. But one time, my friend's mom told me to always say yes when someone is offering you a gift because sometimes it means just as much to the person offering the gift as it does to the person receiving the gift. Gifts aren't really my thing, but that always stuck with me, you know?"

The crosswalk's prerecorded message feels like it's getting louder and louder every time it repeats. It feels like it's screaming at me—and only me—at the moment.

It's happening all over again.

The words are coming out of my mouth faster than I can stop them.

More words bubble up and out of me.

"So I thought to myself, *What would Marley's mom tell me to do right now?* She would tell me to accept the offer and take the pizza, because who knows, you might have wanted me to have that piece of pizza as much as I wanted it! Not that I wanted it so badly I'd pressure you into buying it for me, because I would never do that. No matter how broke I am, I'd never do that. Did you know people do that? They go on dates when they're low on cash just so they can get someone to buy them dinner?"

I am single-handedly ruining this beautiful night with every word that escapes my lips in a violently projectile fashion.

"I could never do that. Not that those people aren't good people because they do that. I'm sure they're great people. If you've done that, I'm sorry. I didn't mean to offend you. All I'm saying is...it doesn't matter how broke I am. You can count on me to pay for my own pizza! Don't you worry about that!"

"And the sex, yes?"

...*The what?*

ROUGE PIÉTON BOULEVARD JOURDAN

"I'm sorry...it sounded like you just said sex."

In an attempt to mask how wildly uncomfortable I am, I'm laughing harder than I should be. I can't tell for sure, but I don't think it's working.

ROUGE PIÉTON BOULEVARD JOURDAN

"Yes, sex. Do you have enough to also pay me for the sex?"

WHY IS HE TALKING ABOUT SEX?

NO ONE IS TALKING ABOUT SEX.

WE HAVE NOT HAD SEX.

WE HAVE NOT TALKED ABOUT HAVING SEX.

WHY IS HE TALKING ABOUT SE—

Oh my god.

Ohmygodohmygodohmygodohmygodohmygodohmygodohmy
godohmygodohmygodohmygodohmygodohmygodohmygodoh
mygodohmygodohmygodohmygodohmygodohmygodOhmygod
ohmygodohmygodohmygodohmyohmygodohmygodohmygodoh
mygodohmygodohmygodohmygodohmygodohmygodohmy
godohmygodohmygodohmygododohmygodohmygod
ohmygodohmygodohmygodohmygodohmygodoh
mygodohmygodohmygodohmygodohmygodohmygod
ohmygodohmygodohmygodohmygodohmygodohmy
godohmygodohmygodohmygodohmygodohmygodoh
mygodohmygodohmygodohmygodohmygodohmygod
ohmygodohmygodohmygodohmygodohmygodohmy
godohmygodohmygodohmygodohmygodohmygod
ohmygodohmygodohmygodohmygodohmygodohmy
godohmygodohmygodohmygodohmygodohmygod
ohmygodohmygodohmygodohmygodohmy
godohmygodohmygodohmgodohmygodohmygod
ohmygodohmygodohmygodohmygodohmy
godohmygodohmygodohmygod
ohmygodohmygodohmygodohmy
godohmygodohmygodohmygodoh
mygodohmygodohmygodohmygodohmy
godohmygodohmygodohmygod
ohmygodohmygodohmygodoh
mygodohmygodohmygodohmy
godohmygodohmygodohmygod
ohmygodohmygodohmygodohmy
godohmygodohmygodohmygod
ohmygodohmygodohmygodoh
mygodohmymygodohmygodohmygod
ohmygodohmygodohmygodoh
mygodohmygodohmygodohmy
godohmygodohmygodoh

mygodohmygodohmygodohmygod
ohmygodohmygodohmygodohmy
godohmygodohmygodohmygodoh
mygodohmygodohmygodohmy
godohmygodohmygodohmygodoh
mygodohmygodohmygodohmygod
ohmygodohmygodohmygodoh
mygodohmygodohmygodohmy
godohmygodohmygodohmygod
ohmygodohmygodohmygodoh
mygodohmygodohmygodohmy
godohmygodohmygodohmygod
ohmygodohmygodohmygodoh
mygodohmygodohmygod
ohmygodohmygodohmy
godohmygodohmygodoh
mygodohmygodohmygod
ohmygodohmygodohmy
godohmygodohmygod
ohmygodohmygodoh
mygodohmgodohmy
godohmygodohmy
godohmygod
ohmygod.

Every human being within earshot of me and White Button-Up is now watching us, waiting for a response from me that *does not exist.* As of right now, I can't imagine a response complete enough to explain what's happening (which is ironic because, just a minute ago, I couldn't shut the fuck up).

But now, roughly a million seconds later, I barely believe I even own vocal cords.

ROUGE PIÉTON BOULEVARD JOURDAN

"I...think...there has been a misunderstanding."

My face is not red. It is officially purple. The skin on my face is so hot that it physically hurts when my mouth moves as I speak. I have never—and I mean never—misunderstood the actions of another human being so tremendously.

"No misunderstanding. I ask if you want company for the night. I told you my rate is cheap. You say yes, and you tell me you'll pay in your room. Where is the misunderstanding?"

"I—oh my god. Oh my god. I am *so sorry.* I have made a huge mistake. When you asked if I wanted company, I had no clue you meant...*COMPANY.* Like"—I look around me and confirm my friends are staring as intensely at us as I figured they were (and hoped they weren't) before I continue—"as in *SEX.*" The word "sex" comes out of my mouth so quietly that it almost sounds like I'm talking and inhaling at the same time.

"So you can't pay?"

"I...I promise, I d-didn't know! I'm not sure I even knew what I was planning on doing when we *got up* to my dorm room! I mean, I figured we would all play board games and drink the beer in our mini-fridge and...and *talk*! I didn't think sex was even—and I *really* didn't think that you were—and I am so, *so sorry* for wasting your time! I can pay you back for the pizza! Please let me pay you back for the pizza!"

DING DING DING DING DING DING.

Oh good, it's finally safe to cross.

My classmates are frozen, clearly unsure of how much or how little of their help to offer me. People on the corner are shoving past them to cross the street.

I'm so overwhelmed by the thought of accidentally wasting an escort's time that it takes *way longer* than it should for every other truth to sink in that comes with accidentally wasting an escort's time.

Little by little, tonight is beginning to make a lot more sense as White Button-Up's face stares angrily back at me.

All the time he spent with me tonight wasn't because he thought I was interesting or pretty.

He didn't buy me a drink because he wanted to get to know me.

He didn't buy me a slice of pizza because I'm someone he sees worthy of a sort-of date.

He didn't hold my hand because he wanted to hold my hand.

Oh my god, I want to vomit at the thought of him holding my hand.

I look up at the sky and try to fill my lungs with air from above my head, hoping it might offer me something that the air just below it couldn't.

In the most beautiful French accent, White Button-Up shouts, *"I don't want your fucking pizza money!"* The intensity in his voice makes me jump, and I feel Stella by my side before the exclamation mark at the end of his sentence. He turns his body around and begins walking away.

Two steps in, he cocks his head to the left and spits on the sidewalk without stopping.

By the tight grip Stella has on my forearm, I can tell she's more nervous than her voice sounds when she says, "I don't want you to take this the wrong way, but...we all thought you knew."

If there's a threshold for how much humiliation the human body can hold inside itself before needing to make room for more, Stella's comment just shoved me right past it. It takes all of five seconds for the entire night *and* that godforsaken pizza to launch out of my stomach and onto the sidewalk.

The bad news—besides the obvious—is: I have terrible aim, and Stella's shoes are ruined forever, no matter how many times she tells me she is an expert at getting stains out.

This isn't a stain.

This is a shoe funeral.

The good news is: I will never accidentally waste a sex worker's time *ever again*. Stella and I update the list of glances just to make sure.

THE WINDOW BACK TO CALIFORNIA

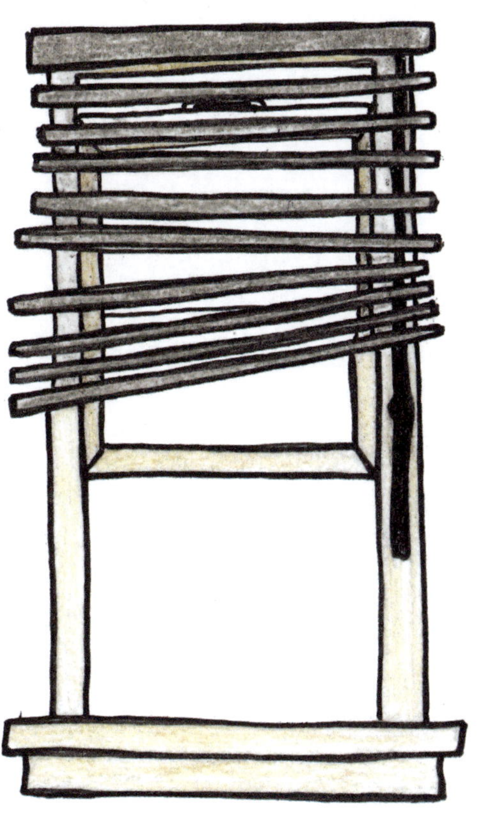

two truths and a lie

1. The sky is blue sometimes. Not always, but sometimes. Every once in a while, the sky transforms itself into a soft sheet of red and orange and pink and purple just before the sun kisses the horizon and says good night until tomorrow. Sometimes the sky becomes gray as it opens itself up and rains on the earth below it. And sometimes the sky turns into a threatening shade of green before tornado sirens begin to ring, creating a slight panic even though maybe you've been living in a place that has tornado sirens long enough to know everything is probably fine. Unless it isn't fine, in which case you'll be worried The Perfect Amount. Not that worrying The Perfect Amount can do anything to help your situation re: The Tornado, but at least you will be panicking accordingly. But then again, it's probably nothing and you're more worried than you need to be. Anyway, the sky is blue sometimes.

2. A boy from my past invited me to meet him at the beach one night and then asked if I was still a virgin no less than five minutes after we hugged and said "Hello, great to see you!" I refused to answer his question, because even though I could tell from the way he asked it that my answer would be the answer he was looking for, my answer was absolutely none of his business. I thought he was going to tell me he liked me Way Back When.

During the thirty-minute drive to the beach, I even thought, *Maybe this is a date? It has all the technical makings of a date, so it wouldn't be crazy to assume this might be a date.* Apparently, he had some Virginity Business to attend to first.

"Why does it matter?" I said as I stepped from one rock to another, trying my best to avoid landing in the puddles that pooled in the grooves of the large rocks along the cliff where he asked me to meet him. The car I drove to the beach wasn't mine, and I would've rather not needed to explain to my mom why the mat under the driver's seat was covered in Beach Mud. Mostly because she didn't know she lent me her car in the first place.

Because I left after she fell asleep.

(This was a coincidence, of course. I didn't plan to leave after she fell asleep just so I could take the keys out of her purse and reverse her car out of the driveway with the headlights strategically turned off so she wouldn't wake up and find out I'd left, just so I could return her keys back to her purse before she woke up with just enough time for me to pretend I was still asleep like I had been "all night." A mere coincidence that my borrowing of her car worked out this way.)

"It matters because it matters!" he said, so much more confidently than he had any right to sound.

He began telling me why my virginity—or possible lack thereof—mattered to him. Why it mattered to a boy from my past I didn't even know well enough anymore to be able to discern if this was a date or not. He told me why it mattered to him and also to every boy and man and boy-man and guyish guy-man-boy on the planet and, because of this, why it should matter to me.

"Women are like roses, full of petals..." he started.

I winced at the comparison and wondered who gave him

this idea and exactly how many times he had recited it to Roses just like me.

At the beach.

At night.

While standing on rocks at the edge of a cliff.

I felt my shoe land in a puddle, and my sock began to soak up as much seawater as it could hold, and then I felt it draw in a little more water after that. I would have taken my shoes off when I arrived at the beach, but I assumed we would walk down the staircase and onto the sand before the subject of my virginity was broached.

I guess not.

Actually, I didn't think my virginity would be a topic of conversation *at all* tonight, or any other night after tonight that I might—but definitely won't—see him again. He spoke with so much confidence that it made me question whether I deserved to be offended by this conversation.

"Oh. That water looks cold. That sucks."

"It's very cold. My sock is all wet."

"Think of yourself as a beautiful rose, and when you are still a virgin, you still have all of your petals—"

"I don't want to think of myself as a rose, Terence. I *especially* don't want *you* thinking of me as a rose either."

"—and you still have *all* of your petals."

"Okay."

"And with all of your petals still in place, you are so beautiful! Exactly as you are meant to be! Full of petals. Untouched. Do you understand what I'm saying?"

"I do. Please stop calling me a rose."

"And every time you give your body to someone, it's like

they're plucking one of your petals off and dropping it on the ground—"

"This is so weird?"

"—they drop it on the ground! Your rose becomes smaller and smaller, and it loses all its beauty. And then on your wedding night—"

I slipped once more, and my dry foot landed in another puddle. Judging by how wet the bottom of my pants leg was, this puddle was much deeper than the first.

I wonder if there were any small crabs or tiny sea creatures living in that puddle.

I wonder if my foot had landed on top of them.

Why aren't there any streetlights lining this road? We're standing next to one of the only staircases that leads down to the beach, so I feel like there should be *at least* one streetlight.

The idea that I might have just killed a small crab makes me want to cry, and my socks are emitting a squishing sound that makes every single one of my steps sound like a practical joke, and I am so cold that I've started to shiver.

"You should take your shoes off if you're going to keep stepping in the water like that. You look cold." He slinks his arms out of his tan Members Only jacket, which looks like it was taken straight off a mannequin at a thrift store. Not the kind of thrift store that's actually thrifty, but the kind of thrift store that doesn't have any price tags because the people who can afford to shop there don't need to bother themselves with price tags.

Once his jacket is all the way off, I think he's going to hand it to me to help me warm up.

But he doesn't hand it to me.

Instead, he ties it around his waist.

"I'm fine, thanks. I think it's weird you feel so invested in my virginity, seeing as it has nothing to do with you. What with all the Rose Petal Collecting and all that."

"You really do look cold."

"I said I'm fine."

"Are you sure?"

"Yes. I'm fine."

I am the definition of Not Fine.

I want to take my wet shoes and socks off *very* much, but I would rather wait until I get closer to my car. The last thing I need is to step on a random piece of glass or a broken seashell—and as a result, be forced to hear any more about my rose petals as I tend to a gash on the heel of my foot.

"And then on your wedding night!" he continues without any hesitation. "When you finally give your rose to your husband forever—"

"Please, stop. I am begging you to stop. If you don't stop, I'm just going to call the police."

I'm not going to call the police, but Terence doesn't need to know that. I stole my mom's car to get here, and the idea of emergency response vehicles makes me nervous. When I was six years old, I called 911 because I convinced a few kids that we could add 911 into a phone number and it wouldn't count as dialing 911. But one single call placed to (714) 911-2345 landed me and my babysitter on the porch of my mom's boyfriend's house, explaining to the police that the call was my fault, and I'd felt brave while waiting next to my mom's boyfriend's children for our Shrinky Dinks to finish cooking in my Easy-Bake Oven.

At this point, I could be having an actual emergency, and I'd reason with myself that it's not worth calling 911 because I don't want to bother them and *it could be so much worse! Why waste their time?*

I hold up my hand like a crossing guard outside of an elementary school as I shake my leg to remove as much excess ocean water from my shoes as I can.

"Don't you want to give your husband a rose with all its petals when you get married?"

I look at the edge of the cliff and imagine walking right off it. That would get me away from this conversation *much* faster than walking to my car. But then my mom might never get her car back, and she loves this car.

"Who says I want to marry a man? Or that I want to get married at all? And who says I care what *anyone*—besides myself—thinks about my rose and all my rose petals? And what about *your* rose? Let's talk about *your* rose for a second!"

"Elyse, it doesn't really work that way—"

"Yeah, I'm sure it doesn't." I cut him off, hoping this will stop him from teaching me any more about this magical metaphor for sex he feels *so* strongly about; that for the sake of all men everywhere, he has taken it upon himself to teach me all about this evening.

Part of me wants to tell him I would have had sex with him in a car tonight, if he only would have asked. Not because I actually would have had sex with him in a car tonight, but because I would have loved to see how many seconds it took for him to teach me all the loopholes that exist in this magical metaphor, depending on who's watching.

I also don't want him to leave this cliff with the pleasure of hearing those words come out of my mouth, especially when I don't mean them.

I am still a virgin after all, petals fully intact.

I hate that I know this metaphor now.

I finally make it across the rocks and back onto the grass where he's standing. I bend down and wring out the bottom of my pants, then untie my shoelaces. I wish I would have planned ahead and put a towel in the trunk, or not have driven to the beach at all.

"Are you leaving?"

"Yes."

"Can I walk you to your car?"

"If I say no, are you just going to walk me to my car anyway?"

"Probably. It's really dark out here."

"All right. Let's go then."

It takes all of thirty seconds for us to reach my car. Sometime between when I unlock the car doors and open the driver's-side door, he shouts loudly, "Let's play a game! The game where we each tell each other something we've never told anyone before!"

His smile makes him look like a serial killer.

"No, thanks. Good night."

I pop the trunk of my mom's car, and I throw my shoes and very wet socks into the back before closing it way too loudly.

"Do you know what a Fleshlight is?"

I pretend I didn't hear his absurd question and climb into the car. I cannot physically handle being here any longer or I am going to say something I regret. At best, I heard his question wrong. At worst, I heard his question right and tonight is about to take its second turn into conversational territory I'm beyond uncomfortable exploring with him.

"Goodbye, Terence."

"That's my confession!" he says. "I have a Fleshlight. Do you know what a Fleshlight is?"

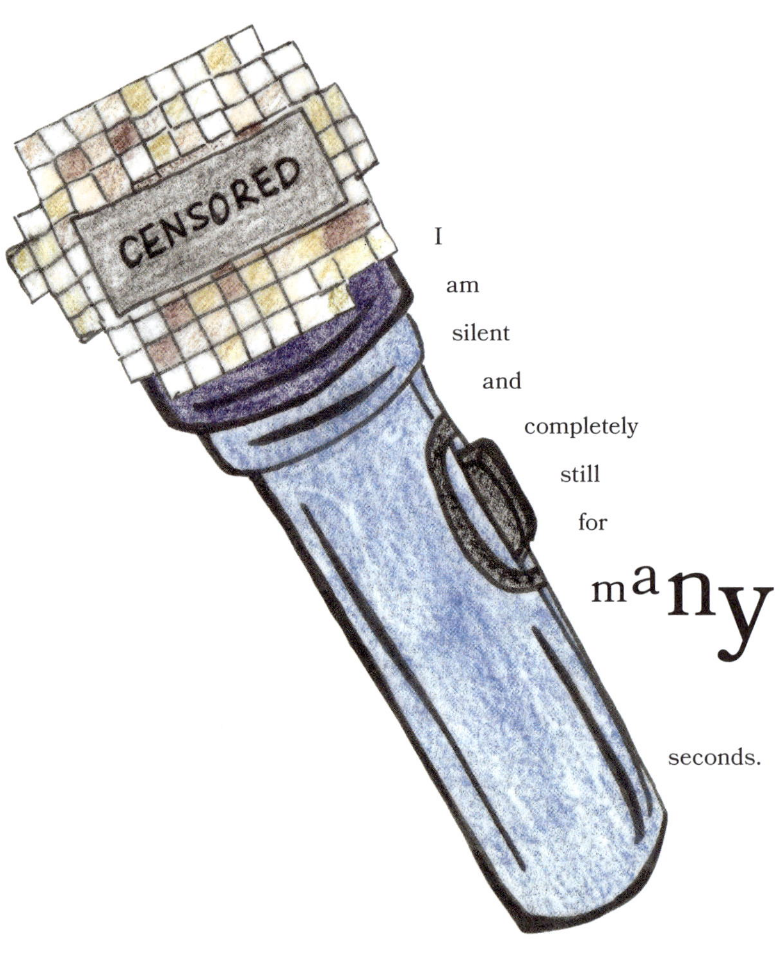

I

am

silent

and

completely

still

for

many

seconds.

And then laughter explodes out of my mouth as he watches me lose the last of my self-control. He looks back at me as if what he just confessed isn't the most absurd fun fact he could shout at me after he just spent the entire evening telling me how sacred and important my sexual purity is to him and all mankind. For him to punctuate his unrelenting and unsolicited advice regarding my own virtue with a confession about owning a pretend flashlight that he can discreetly masturbate into makes more sense than I ever want it to.

It makes more sense than it ever should.

"Oh yes," I manage to say through tears and laughter that I refuse to disguise any longer this evening. "Yes, I know what a Fleshlight is. And just to confirm, you *did* say Fleshlight, correct? You didn't say 'flashlight.' You said Fleshlight. *F-L-E-S-H*-light. Fleshlight." I spell his confession out as plainly and evenly as I can before I say anything more.

"Yes, that's right. Okay, your turn! Tell me something you've never told anyone before."

I take multiple deep breaths and steady myself before speaking again.

"Something I've never told anyone...hmm..." I do my best to take my time and look as though I am in deep thought. I hum thinking noises in the back of my throat, and I stare purposefully at my hands as they trace the stitching on the steering wheel in front of me. I stare off into the distance, then turn to Terence. "Mmm...okay, I've got one!"

Terence rubs his hands together as if the memory of whatever I'm about to confess is going to taste delicious as he kills me on this dark, oceanside cliff and then eats my body to get rid of the evidence.

"Something I've never told anyone." I blink and try not to smile. "I don't ever want to hear about your Fleshlight ever again, and I hope that if you ever think of me while using it, you immediately go soft and lose your ability to finish. And I hope that you tell your future wife all about your Fleshlight immediately after you ask her if she's a virgin. So there you go! A bunch of things I have *never* told anyone before! Good night!"

I *finally* force the car door closed and drive away as fast as I possibly can. I have not seen or heard from Terence since, but I sincerely hope Terence and his Fleshlight and his wife are very happy together.

Yes, Terence is married! Congrats, Terence!

And finally, number three:

3. All the blood in my body was replaced with cold-pressed organic apple juice when I was seven years old and I never bothered to change it back.

Okay, time to guess!
Which one is the lie?

Have you ever wondered what it's like to date a poet?

The date is going far better than either of them expected. He pulls her chair out for her before she sits down. She compliments his tie. They order food that they can eat without Slurping or Spilling. Things they won't have to pick up with their hands and that won't make their breath smell like anything other than Breath.

"I'll skip the garlic," she says through a mild laugh while ordering. "Unless you're having garlic too, of course!" she adds quickly.

"I like garlic," he replies.

Neither of them speaks about garlic for the rest of the evening.

They order their Garlic-less meals and tear off pieces of bread from the complimentary loaf sitting in the middle of the table. Their waitress made special mention of the bread's endless refills while setting it down, as if to distinguish this restaurant from any other that provides bread for the table.

He looks down at his water glass, which is sweating into the tablecloth. "If we ate all this bread, do you think they would give us more?"

She feels proud to have the answer to his question. "I believe so, yes. The waitress *did* say that the bread was endless."

He holds the wire bread basket in his hands. "How many times do you think they would give us more bread if we ask for it?"

He is speaking directly to the bread.

"As many times as we ask, I would assume."

"But how *much* bread do you think they would give us? Surely they would stop refilling our empty bread basket at a certain point. There's only so much bread in this restaurant. Eventually this restaurant will run out of bread. There's no way they would allow us to eat *all the bread* they have, just because we ask for it. That would be insane. Don't you agree? That it would be insane?"

He looks at her, waiting for a response. As if he didn't just spend the last minute and a half questioning the hypothetical boundaries of Endless Bread.

"That...*would* be insane, yes—"

"I mean, *imagine* if we ate every single piece of bread in this restaurant and then two people walked in right after we left. They'd probably be on a date just like us! What if they wanted a basket of bread? What would the restaurant say? 'No, I'm sorry. The couple that sat here before you *ate all of it*'? There's no way they're baking bread back there! We'll be lucky if they even microwave our dinner all the way. Fresh bread!? Are you kidding me? Do you know how *insane* that would be? The idea of endless anything, *especially bread*, is absolutely absurd. Endless Anything doesn't exist! Nothing is *Endless*!"

The date is no longer going as well as it once was.

It's also not going as badly as it will.

The waitress delivers their carefully selected meals to the table.

Garlic-less, and most definitely not Endless.

It would be in everyone's best interest if no one mentioned Endless Anything for the rest of the night.

"Would you like more bread to eat with your dinner?" The waitress, dressed in all black, gestures toward the empty basket. Neither of them answers.

I would be happy if I never saw a basket of bread for the rest of my life, she thinks.

Her food looks better. I knew I should have ordered something else, he thinks at the same time.

Arms dressed in black remove the Endless Bread from the table, and they eat their meals in silence. The date is officially going as bad as it could go.

She's happy she drove herself here.

He's thinking about the traffic waiting for him on the freeway.

He asks for the check.

She insists on splitting the bill.

He refuses.

She relents.

She drives home, wondering how the night went so wrong so quickly.

She climbs into bed. The two glasses of red wine she drank when she walked into her apartment are causing the ceiling to move without her permission. She falls asleep wondering if she's too picky, if she'd been expecting too much from a blind date. It was just a heated debate about Endless Bread, after all. Is that really so bad?

She would give *anything* to care about *something* as much as he cared about that bread basket.

Sleep finds her quickly.

Seven hours and two years pass. Morning light is pouring through the blackout curtains her coworker swore would change her life. Nothing has changed about her life except that she has new curtains now. They were three times the price and work about half as well as the curtains she had before.

Of course she won't share that with her coworker.

Not even if she asks.

She wakes up to find an email among other emails. This one is different. This one looks worth reading, while the others are coupons and discount codes for Other Things that might change her life.

This email is from a friend she used to know.

Sometime, long ago, in Her Past Life. She refers to anything that happened before her move to Seattle as Her Past Life. She thinks it's subtle enough to serve as an inside joke she can keep between herself and no one else. Everyone knows what she means, and she smiles secretly every time she says it.

The email is open now, and she stares at its contents. She is confused.

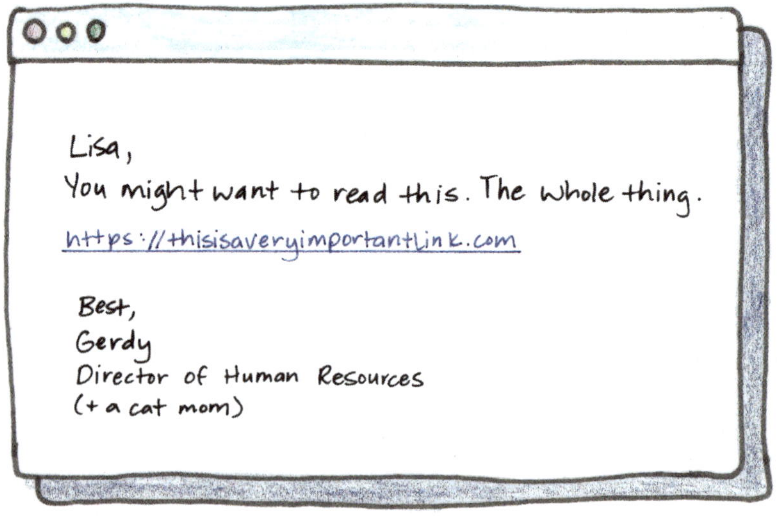
Lisa,
You might want to read this. The whole thing.
https://thisisaveryimportantlink.com

Best,
Gerdy
Director of Human Resources
(+ a cat mom)

When she clicks on the link, it takes her to a collection of poems published by a man whose name sounds like someone she went on a date with in Her Past Life. Though...the more she reads, the more it sounds nothing at all like the date she was on, two years and some change ago.

```
The poems are about a woman who loved garlic.
Whose breath was on fire.
Who couldn't stop talking about bread.
Whose compliments were lacking.
Whose thoughts weren't tracking.
Who forced him to pay and then fled.
```

Pages and pages and pages of poems.

So many poems.

All of them are written about a woman resembling her in every single way except the truth.

"How could you do this?" she asks him, a stranger from Her Past Life who cares too much about Endless Bread, in an email.

"How could I do what?" he replies in a phone call.

"The poems! You wrote those about me! And you wrote me exactly as I wasn't!"

"None of those poems are about you. I barely even know you. Could you imagine barely knowing someone and writing a poem about them?"

"But that's exactly what you did! The only way those poems could be *more* about me is if you titled every single one of them *LISA: THE ONE FROM BACK THEN!*"

"Lisa, is it? Great to meet you, Lisa. That would—"

"We've already met! You just *called* me! What are you talking about!?"

"What I was saying was...that would be *absurd*, Lisa. I've never written a single poem about you. I've never written a poem at all. I simply capture universal human experiences by painting the written word onto empty pages and allow others to interpret them as they please. If you would like to interpret the words I write as a poem about you, then go right ahead. But I can assure you that any resemblance between you and my words...it's all a mere coincidence, Lisa. If you were honest with yourself, you might see that your inflated ego is causing *you* to read *yourself* into my *art*."

"BUT I'M NOT THE ONE WHO WOULDN'T SHUT UP ABOUT THE BREAD!"

"Why are you shouting? And who said anything about the bread?"

"You did! In your poem! And for, like, *half* of our date!"

"Lisa, wherever you think we went together...that was *not* a date. Besides, I don't even like bread. Have you ever considered that bread isn't always bread? That dinner isn't always a date? Maybe bread represents a person—a person that isn't *you*. Honestly, Lisa, maybe the problem here is that you don't understand art. Have you ever stopped and considered that you don't understand art?"

Maybe he is right.

Maybe she *doesn't* understand art.

The more she thinks about it, the more she's convinced she doesn't understand much of *anything at all*.

She reads the poems over and over, just to ensure that she understands exactly as little as she does. She remains just angry enough, and definitely more angry than she's comfortable admitting. Especially when she's reading poems that aren't even about her.

He said they weren't—so they *must* not be.

It's a shame she doesn't understand art.

She loves it so much.

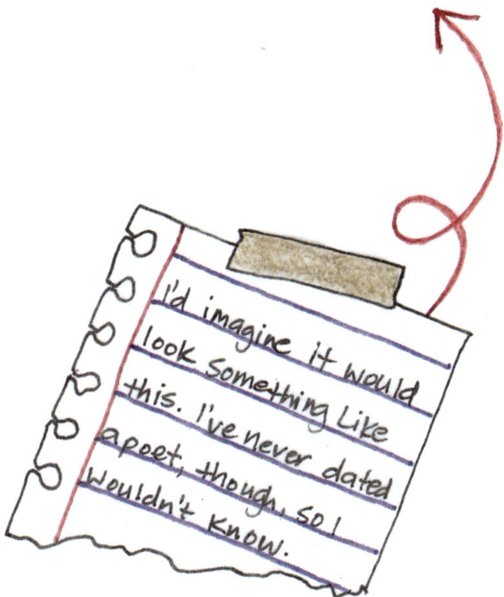

His + Hers

He sprayed His cologne onto
me and then packed me into His bag.
I was next to a shoebox that housed many other things.
everything except shoes.
too many things for such a small shoebox.

when She saw me, She cried.
Her face looked happy
and Her voice sounded sad.
way too sad.
definitely more sad than Her face looked happy.

He said I was Hers.
He wanted Her to keep me.
I was His and now I'm Hers.
I know Her as well as He knows Her,
and We don't know Her as well as We used to.

I've been hers before, but never *Hers.*
countless hers have borrowed me.
He's taken me back just as many times.

I've belonged to Him for So Many Years.
more than five and less than one hundred.
a number falling somewhere in between those two,
making the number of years *exactly* So Many.

Her arms slid through my arms.
I rested on top of Her white t-shirt.
His hands slowly buttoned my bottomest button.
He buttoned my second-bottomest button even slower.
She buttoned my third all by Herself.

no more buttons were buttoned after that.
His hands ran down the length of Our plaid arms.
He told Her I was a perfect fit.
She agreed.

the shoebox spilled open inside His bag.
too many things were mixing at the bottom.
He showed them to Her one at a time.

a piece of paper, folded in half.
He unfolded it to show Her the inside two halves.
She laughed and held the hidden halves against Her chest and me.
She read the words on the hidden halves and stopped laughing.

a small bottle of His cologne.
He sprayed it in the air to show Her how it works.
He showed Her what the spray bottle does.
it sprayed. She nodded.

a book He used to write in.
all the pages were white when We bought the book.
only some of all the pages are fully white anymore.
He tells Her to fill the rest of all the pages with whatever She wants.

one at a time, He continued to show Her too many things.
too many things that belonged to Him this morning.
too many things that belong to Her tonight.

and every night after tonight.

and every tonight after that.

too many things made Her cry again.
He asked Her to stop crying and She said She couldn't,
so He cried too.
just barely.
just enough to count.

His bag was empty.
He looked at Her and then looked at Us together.
He held my blue and green in His hands as He told Her too much.

He told Her that I've always belonged to Her.
that He's only been borrowing me.
that He wants to, won't, and can't ever belong to Her.
that I will always be what He cannot.

Hers.

So Many Years of borrowing and belonging.

So Many Years of His and Hers,
with a million his and hers in between.
He left with an empty bag,
while I stayed being Hers.

So Many Years with Her

started three years ago.

the white t-shirt She wore when I stopped being His
lies lost in the bottom of a drawer.
a gray t-shirt has taken its place on Her body
but I have stayed where They put me.
I have stayed on Her.

My blue and green swallow Her.
She wraps Our arms around Her chest.
She tells me that I'm not Him, but I used to be His.
that I'm something She has never and won't ever be.
that She pretends She's just borrowing me.
that She hates Him for making me Hers.
that all She wants is to be wanted by Him.
that wanting Him will go away.
that this is for the best.
this will get easier.
this isn't getting any easier.
this will never get any easier.

I used to be His,
now I am Hers.
They will never be Theirs.
I think I will always be both.

THE LADDER TO AUSTRALIA

Meat Cute

"Is it possible that you're overthinking this?"

I'm standing in front of a wall of nuts. Some roasted and some not. The length of time they've been roasted varies slightly from bin to bin. I wasn't even aware this mattered to me until I was offered a slightly less roasted cashew than the cashews I'd previously planned on purchasing when I walked into this grocery store. Until now I've been perfectly fine with a cashew roasted The Normal Amount.

"It is possible, yes."

I fill a bag with cashews that are roasted more than Slightly and less than All The Way. Evan is watching me carefully make my selection with more curiosity on his face than I'm comfortable with. I ask him if he needs anything while we're in the nut aisle, trying my hardest to provide him with as little fuel as possible for the inappropriate joke I'm sure he's already working on.

To my surprise, he suppresses the joke.

I realize I don't know Evan very well outside of the few band rehearsals we've both been a part of. I know he's Australian. And I also know he isn't an asshole and he has a car. That's about as much as I need to know when accepting a free ride from another student that keeps me from being late.

I walk toward the meat counter to gather the other half of my dinner: a kilo of sliced roast beef that I intend on eating with my hands straight out of the bag and in a hurry.

Of all the ways one could enjoy a two-pound bag of sliced roast beef, Forkless and In A Rush feels like the most correct way. I am a firm believer that roast beef would agree with me, if it could speak. But it doesn't speak.

It's roast beef.

That would be ridiculous.

I take a ticket with the number fifty-six printed on it, securing my place in an invisible line made up of imaginary people at the meat counter. I look at the slip of paper in my hands and think of the delicious dinner that's currently sitting on my kitchen counter, waiting to cool down enough to be covered with a lid and thrown into my backpack.

(The same dinner that made me late after I promised Evan I would have more than enough time to make it.)

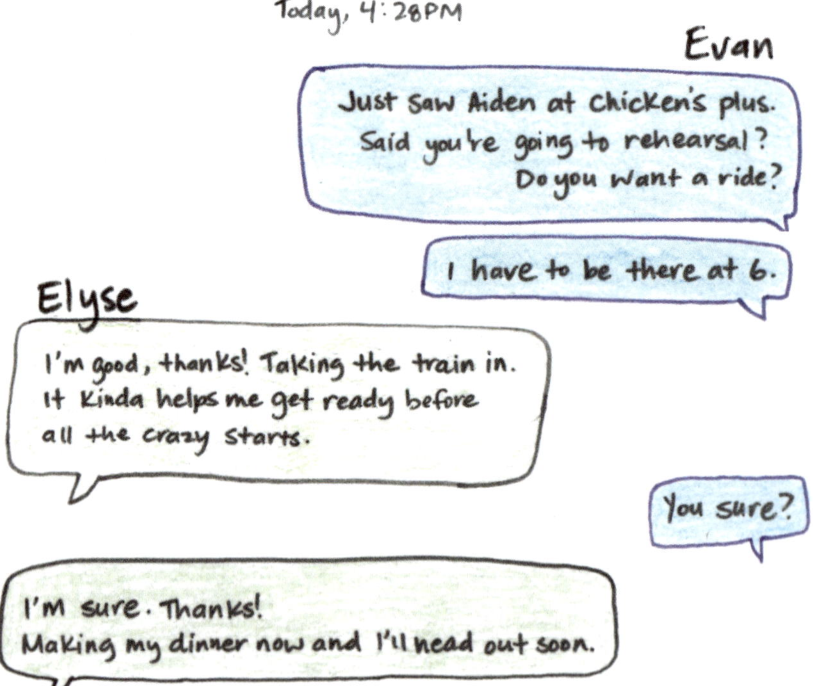

Mate you're gonna be late.

What do you think I should do with all the extra time I'll have after I'm done cooking this chicken + broccoli?

Miss your train, I reckon.

It's like you don't believe in me at all.

Sorry.

I *believe* you are going to miss your train.

Today, 5:02 PM

Have you left your flat yet? I think I'm going to miss my train.

The good news is that my homemade dinner is definitely cool enough for its lid. The bad news is it's also very much still at home, forgotten on my kitchen counter.

I look at the meat behind the counter and begin to wonder how long cooked food remains safe to eat without refrigeration. I decide to find out when I get home by eating my forgotten dinner and waiting to see if I get sick. I volunteer my body to participate in scientific research like this more often than I am willing to admit.

"NUMBER FORTY-*TWO*?"

The Man Behind The Counter shouts so much louder than would *ever* be necessary, and it temporarily distracts me from just how many numbers exist between forty-two and fifty-six. There isn't a soul in this grocery store besides me, Evan, the butcher, and one cashier at the front. I look around, and Forty-Two is nowhere to be found.

"NUMBER FORTY-*THREE*?"

He is looking directly at me. I take his eye contact as a challenge and engage in a very bizarre staring contest that I'm not entirely sure is one-sided. It seems as though Forty-Three and Forty-Two have left the building together. Their meat? Entirely unpurchased.

I see two men approaching out of the corner of my eye.

"Hey, bro," Evan says to the one on the right as I turn to look at everyone. "Hey, man," he says to the other.

Bro reaches out to engage in the Slapshug™. This is a greeting that usually starts as a low high five, which transitions into a handshake and ends somewhere in the neighborhood of a one-armed hug and a very loud slap on the back.

"NUMBER FORTY-*FOUR*?"

Bro releases Evan from their embrace, and Man forgoes the ritual entirely by simply waving. I'm slightly disappointed that I don't get another chance to study the ceremonial greeting but equally grateful I don't have to stand there awkwardly while it happens.

"Elyse, this is Josh," Evan says, gesturing to Bro, "and this is Jonas," gesturing to Man.

I lift my hand in the air to say hello and offer my name once more, even though Evan already said it.

"NUMBER FORTY-*FIVE*?"

"Josh and Jonas—you really have the whole alliteration thing going for you guys."

Jonas laughs. I consider going into a joke about how they probably pick their friends exclusively on the basis of alliteration, hoping one day to redeem the whole J-Name Thing. I was *thisclose*.

And then I consider the fact that they might not even know about the whole J-Name Thing, which means I would be forced to explain the general distrust for men whose names start with the letter *J*. I don't understand it either, I just read it in a book somewhere when I was a teenager...and the longer I think about it, the more I'm convinced I shouldn't say it.

It just feels like second conversation material.

Not that there will be a second conversation.

"Yeah, I actually only make friends with people whose names start with the letter *J*," Jonas says, stealing the words right out of my head.

"Oh my god, I was going to—"

"NUMBER FORTY-*SIX*?"

"What about me?" Evan asks Jonas. I realize just now that my and Evan's name both start with the letter *E*, but I refuse to say anything else about alliteration. Aloud or otherwise.

The Man Behind The Counter calls numbers forty-seven through fifty-five. Somewhere in between, Jonas and I fall into a comfortable conversation perfectly parallel to Evan and Josh's. We talk about the only thing we have in common besides being American, which is school. Specifically, the classes I didn't know we shared. There is nothing remarkable about our conversation, other than that small talk seems easier with him than it does with others. I ask questions and he answers them. He asks the same questions in return. We do all the things two people do in a typical conversation.

Things I usually work very hard to remember to sprinkle into social interactions.

Things Jonas seems to do without even thinking.

I'm usually unable to pay attention in situations like this, especially if another conversation is happening just an arm's length away. Too many sounds. Too many lights that are Too White and Too Bright. Altogether, there are Too Many Toos in this grocery store. I shouldn't be able to focus on what Jonas is saying, considering all the aforementioned Toos.

But I'm focusing just fine and enjoying myself as much as any other person might enjoy making a new acquaintance.

(Which would probably surprise me if I were to stop and think about it.)

(But I'm not going to stop and think about it.)

"NUMBER FIFTY-*SIX*?"

The Man Behind The Counter is staring at me.

Five minutes ago, I had no feelings at all about ordering my kilo of roast beef. Now, in front of this small audience that has assembled itself by the meat counter, I'm slightly more aware of my dinner selection than I'd like to be. I pretend I'm as confident as I was when I walked into the grocery store.

"A kilo of roast beef, please. Thinly sliced, if possible?"

"Making a bunch of sandwiches?" Jonas asks, trying to fill the space in our conversation that has been created by roast beef.

"Something like that!" I nod my head so violently that even I'm unsure of what I'm doing or why I'm doing it so...

...gigantically.

"Actually…no, sorry. That was a lie. I'm just eating this right out of the bag. Probably all of it. I didn't need to tell you that last part. Not that I *shouldn't* have told you that last part. But if I didn't, I'd feel like I was lying. Sometimes just the feeling that I might be lying without trying to lie makes my stomach hurt. So…just to be clear, I'm going to eat this entire bag of roast beef and then a good portion of these cashews that are Slightly Roasted, not to be confused with All The Way Roasted…"

I'm not sure why I'm going into such explicit detail about the plans I have for the food I'm holding. It's food. The "eating of it" is fairly safe to assume.

I notice that Josh and Evan are no longer chatting beside us. I can see Josh wandering off with his empty handbasket and stopping right in front of an endcap display for two-dollar digestive biscuits (Australia's version of graham crackers). He's just far enough away from Jonas and me that we have the illusion of privacy, though his frequent glances back in our general direction tell me we have none. Not that I want any. When I make eye contact with him, Josh suddenly picks up a package of biscuits and studies them as if he's never seen them before. Not just digestive biscuits—packages of food in general.

He is officially a Suspicious Amount of Interested in those biscuits.

As for Evan, I can't find him at all. Given his height, he should be difficult to lose. I look at my watch and note that I have only a few minutes left before I need to run across the street and check in for rehearsal.

When I finally return my attention to Jonas, I'm surprised to find him looking at me.

Has he been looking at me the whole time?

"Sorry. Would you...like some?" I gesture toward Jonas with the meat, neatly wrapped in butcher paper, and the large bag of cashews. I'd like to think I'm so hungry and tired that I'm doing things I normally wouldn't do.

Unfortunately, I'm *just* self-aware enough to know that isn't true at all.

"I'm good. Thanks, though. I need to buy some salami for pasta salad. Me and Josh are having some people over tonight." He turns to gesture toward his friend but makes the same discovery I made a few moments ago.

Josh is no longer there.

Jonas turns farther and finds Josh fiercely examining the endcap display. The pair share a glance that looks more like an inside joke than a smile.

Jonas turns back around and looks directly at me.

"Pasta salad is my contribution. I was putting everything together and realized I forgot to buy the most important ingredient."

"You consider salami the most important ingredient for pasta salad?"

"Of course!"

"Wouldn't the most important ingredient be the...pasta?"

"The pasta is a given. The *salami* is what makes it special."

Suddenly I don't feel as self-conscious about all the roast beef talk. Jonas tells the Man Behind The Counter what he wants. I...didn't realize you could do that without taking a number, but all right.

As Jonas is being handed his order, Evan finally returns to my side.

"I thought you didn't need anything. Where'd you go?"

"We gotta go, mate. Rehearsal starts in, like, two minutes. I didn't drive you all the way out here for food to make you late twice."

Evan's accent makes the emphasis he placed on the word "twice" sound like it splits the word in half and is now two completely separate words.

TUHH—WHYYYEECE.

Getting a ride meant I was given an extra forty minutes I wouldn't have had if I took public transportation to get here. I hadn't planned on spending all forty of my minutes in this grocery store.

"Right. We gotta go. Good to meet you, Jonas." I wave, unsure of the proper protocol for saying "good to meet you" at the end of a conversation instead of the beginning. Usually "good to meet you" is accompanied by a handshake. What about when I'm also saying goodbye? A handshake feels strictly like "hello" territory.

I'll stick with the wave. It feels less Business Meeting and more Enjoy Your Pasta Salad, Kind Stranger!

I offer a wave to Josh as well, and then shout over a gigantic bin of apples. "It was good to meet you! Bye!"

"See you later, mate." Evan pats Jonas on the shoulder.

I wonder how close they all are.

I wonder if they think I'm dating Evan.

I quickly pay for my things at the self-checkout kiosk and begin power walking toward my college campus across the street.

"You two seemed to get on great," Evan says.

"Who? Me and your friend?"

We carefully avoid stepping in the dried oil stains of the parking lot we're cutting through to save some time. I refuse to run because that would mean I'm accepting that I made myself late...again. Which by now I have.

By one minute.

"No, you and the butcher, Elyse." Evan laughs as he steps into the street and we begin to cross.

“Stop, that’s not funny.” I hit the side of his arm and regret it as soon as my hand makes contact. I’d meant it to be a much lighter hit than it ended up being. Evan winces for additional sympathy. “Sorry, Jesus. Sorry. I just meant—I have a boyfriend, and I feel inclined to add that he makes me very happy. Besides, what was I supposed to do? Stand there in silence and stare at my feet while you and your other friend talked about the drums? I was just being nice. I...was nice, right? I think I talked too much about my food.”

We’re walking up to the glass doors of the auditorium. Just before either of us opens the door to go inside, Evan puts his hands in the air. “Was just joking, mate. Yeah, you were nice. Let’s get inside. We’re late.”

“We’re not late...we’re barely late.”

more

she is happy that he's happy, and happy is all she needs.
anything More than happy is *More*, and she's careful not
to ask for More because More is too much.

whatever she's missing isn't missing at all.
she sees the empty spaces where More belongs, and she decided
when she met him that filling all that empty space would be
More than she wants to want.

she is happy!
she is content!
she has *him!*

she doesn't need to want More
  or think about wanting More,
    or even consider wanting to *want* More.
      she can't even imagine More,

                really!

that would be ridiculous,
considering how perfectly happy she is.

he wants More because: More is just enough.
not More from her, of course, because she makes him happy.
More from everything else, and everything that isn't her.

she just wants him, because: More is too much.
he is *just* enough, and everything else that isn't him is More.
More would be More than she needs.

they take turns painting pictures of the future with their words,
sending dreams of forever,
and one day,
across nine thousand miles.

she *can't even tell!*

there's an ocean between their bedrooms.

and she *doesn't even notice!*

every
single
one
of
the
fourteen
hours
that
lives
between
both
of
their
clocks.

she is so happy,
that she has no words at all when he asks her how happy she is,
or what she thinks about the *what-ifs*
they both hope will eventually grow into *whens*.

she is so happy,
that any More would feel impossible.
she doesn't even acknowledge that More exists!

she can't.
she isn't able to.
she won't try.

(please don't ask her to try.)

she is so happy that he's kind,
and honest,
and beautiful,
and hers,
and everything
she
wants
to
want,

which means the exact same thing as:
everything she wants.

she cannot fathom asking for any More.
she is so happy that she cries when he tells her he loves her.

that she preserves his gifted keepsakes
underneath her bed
where they will be safe.
and she can't see them.

that she writes lists in her diary
of all the reasons why they make sense together
and then reads them to herself
so she can memorize them when people ask.

that dreaming of their future
feels like so much More
than she might ever be able to handle.

look at her,
she's drowning in all of this

happiness.

Maeve: 37 years old, cake decoration. Loves traveling. Airline industry, events + sales.

Thomas: 47 years old. Hospitality. Creative advertising. Hotel security. Night Audit (= overnight shift for balancing money, guest services overnight, admin tasks.) $

Layla: Night Audit

Brynn: Great at breaking things.

Tabitha: wanted to work in hotels since age 15. likes to teach people things. started working in hotels after school. Boutique hotels is passion. Not chain hotels. Gymnastics and Ice skating. Limbs got too long.

Weston: Hotels for 8 years. Job is in Night Audit.

Mia: similar to Tabitha. 2 placements in 2 hotels. kitchen. Fiji. social work. Prisons. Hotels. Hotel management. studying ~~bu~~ ~~busi~~ ~~bus~~ business in school. Likes sour candy (!!!)

Simon: Loves going to the gym. Ballroom dancer. Professional + very comfortable. Feels safe to be around.

Double beds and up = corporate rooms.

when upgrading guests = <u>Do Not</u> upgrade to better room type (just upgrade to a higher floor.)

IN-HOUSE CALL: "Good Morning / afternoon / evening, this is reception." OR "this is Elyse..."

* uniform is laundered 2x a week. show up in casual clothes and then change when you get here!

after 6 months - staff stays free one night! → $99 staff night → $129 friends + family.

When Things Go Without Saying

"You left your notebook here last night at the front desk. I put it in your box so no one would read it."

"I *knew* I was forgetting something last night! Thank you! I'll go grab it so—"

"So you can take notes?"

Tabitha is staring at me as if she's trapped me in a lie or waiting for me to confess to a crime I don't remember committing.

"Yes. Is that okay?"

"Do you ever take notes on any of the work? Or is it just *us* that you write about in your notebook?"

Oh shit.

Oh shit.

Oh shit oh shit oh shit oh shit oh shit oh shit oh shit.

Well, I guess that explains the look on Tabitha's face.

"I promise it's not what you think."

"I think you're taking notes on me. Am I wrong?"

I try to recall what was written in the notebook I left behind or what Tabitha might have seen when she found it. My mind is in a race with my emotions and Embarrassment is winning. I'm trying to remember what I wrote in my notebook last night, but I can't see it in my mind.

"Why are you taking notes on us? And why did *mine* say…hold on, let me make sure I get this right…" She pulls her phone out of the World's Smallest Pocket, which we have in all our pencil skirts. I dread putting on this part of the uniform but enjoy wearing it once I manage to zip it up.

I'm curious about how Tabitha got her regular-size phone into the World's Smallest Pocket in the first place. I have to hide my phone in my bra or else I can't breathe. The World's Smallest Pocket doesn't even fit the master key card I've tried to keep tucked away in there on multiple occasions.

Tabitha reads the notes she found about herself in my notebook from her phone: "'Gymnastics and Ice-Skating. Limbs got too long'…What *the fuck,* Elyse?"

There is a Very Normal and Not Weird answer to Tabitha's question, but the way I'm oozing panic is not helping my case at all. "First of all…I didn't write anything down that you didn't tell me yourself."

"I think I would remember saying something about my own long limbs."

"Tabs. You literally said to me, *and I quote…*" Very unnaturally, I slide into my pathetic attempt at an Australian accent: *"Elyse, I used to be really into gymnastics and ice-skating. But then my limbs got too long and I had to stop…"*

The longer I try to speak in Tabitha's accent, the worse the accent gets. The worse my accent gets, the more it sounds like mocking—the bullying kind, not the endearing kind. (Though if you ask me, those are the exact same thing, and I don't like either kind.)

I begin recounting Tabitha's story back to her. The same story she told me last night while hunched over our shared computer at the front desk while she taught me how to assign rooms to the housekeeping staff.

Her story went something like this: Tabitha grew up watching Olympic figure skaters on television. Her bedroom walls were lined with figure skating posters and pictures and motivational quotes, all serving as a constant reminder that she *would* become the very thing she wanted to be when she grew up: an Olympic figure skater. She learned how to ice-skate *"minutes"* after she took her first steps in the living room of her childhood home. Right away, she was much better than anyone else her age. She was *"Special"* and *"Excellent"* and *"had Olympic potential."*

Tabitha was put on a fast track for greatness.

But as she got older, she hit an unexpected growth spurt. Her limbs grew *"too much, too quick,"* and her mind struggled to accommodate all her new, added length. *"Overnight,"* her body felt like a stranger. *"Puberty can be a death sentence to a young skater."*

Tabitha was forced to relearn movements that were fundamental and routine. In the process, she injured herself. Tabitha recovered, was rehabilitated, and then injured herself again—the second time much worse than the first. She sustained a career-ending injury to her back and knee.

I close my eyes as if being unable to see would help me remember Tabitha's words from last night even more clearly. I try to quote the last part of our conversation verbatim. "You said, *'And that's when I learned that no matter how good you are at something, being good isn't always enough. My body decided for me that it wasn't built to support my dreams and all the dreams that people gave me. There will always be factors out of your control, and sometimes, being the best has nothing to do with why it doesn't work out.'*...Or something like that."

I notice I've unintentionally started standing like Tabitha, resting all my weight onto my right hip. I shift my weight back to the center. I'm speaking as quickly as I can, afraid to lose momentum and Tabitha's focus.

"The best part was that you didn't even realize what you said! I could see it on your face! You were barely paying attention to your own words. You were staring at the computer as you were speaking, and you kept trailing off in the middle of your sentences. It's like I got punched in the face with wisdom by someone who was sleepwalking. Or—no, actually—it was like someone was giving a life-changing TED Talk, but they were giving it from their bed at midnight and dozing off every few words. I didn't have enough time to write all of that down. But I *did* have enough time to quickly write 'Gymnastics and ice-skating. Limbs got too long.' In my mind, that's basically the same thing."

Tabitha looks more confused than anything else, struggling to process the firehose of information I just blasted her with. "Did I really say all that?"

"Yes! You did!"

Tabitha remains silent for a few moments. I'm convinced she is going to report me to human resources and I will be fired by the end of the day. There is no way I'm walking out of here with a job.

"I should be a life coach."

That is the opposite of what I thought she was going to say.

Tabitha laughs quietly. I can see her expression change slowly as she remembers our conversation from last night. I don't know her well enough to explain how badly I needed to hear what she shared with me. A lot of people give me a lot of different advice, most of it from a very high horse.

Like, the highest horse.

Why is that horse so high?

I don't know.

But it's *up there.*

"It was *really* inspirational, Tabs. That's why I wrote it down…in a very bizarre, abridged shorthand that looks *really* suspicious when you're reading it out of context."

The short answer for why I take notes like this is: People confuse me.

Being around people just for the sake of being around people drains the life out of me, but learning people doesn't drain me nearly as much. Making small notes and reframing the way I think about social interactions has helped me get better at something I am naturally very terrible at:

People.

Even though I prefer being alone, I want my introversion to be a choice I make. I don't want to feel trapped by it. Sometimes I feel very trapped by it.

Is it bizarre that I have all these notes about my coworkers written down on a physical piece of paper? Yes. It sounds a little bit like Serial Killer Behavior if you don't have any context. But is it really so different from putting someone's birthday in your calendar? Or making mental notes (which stay mental and never get written into a notebook!) about someone's favorite ice cream flavor? The notes I take when I'm starting a new job are always about the people I work with. The job will sort itself out.

Take what's happening this morning as an example:

Tabitha is currently in the middle of teaching me how to fold Hospital Corners when making up a guest's bed. This is something housekeeping taught me how to do two days ago. But the very first day I met Tabitha, she told me she likes teaching. *"In another life,*

I would have been a teacher." I made it my mission to allow her to teach me as many things as she wants to teach me, regardless of whether it has anything to do with my job or not.

I will never forget how to make a bed with Hospital Corners ever again, *for the rest of my life*. Even when I *want* to forget about Hospital Corners, because every time I make my bed after learning how to make a bed with Hospital Corners, it never looks complete, and sometimes I just don't have *time* for Hospital Corners because life gets busy and I consider myself lucky if my sheets are clean enough to be on the bed in the first place.

The Job itself, whatever job it is, isn't the hard part for me. I have a specific set of skills (I can pour coffee and say hello to people when they walk by me). I take a job that requires those specific skills. Then I trade my time at that job for money. I trade money for a place to live and food to eat. All of that makes sense to me.

But there are unspoken social contracts within a workplace that—by some miracle—everyone else already understands, and I don't. This Understanding seems baked into others' DNA in a way I can't replicate with *any* amount of trying. When things Go Without Saying, they Never Get Said, and sometimes people need you to Say Those Things So They Understand What The Hell Is Going On.

So a few years ago, I became Just The Right Amount of Observant. The idea that I could learn how to Be Someone Who Understands by becoming Just The Right Amount of Observant was life-changing for me.

I started taking notes everywhere I went. Work, not work...that pretty much covers everywhere, I think. I started to notice—***bvvvrrrrrrrrb***

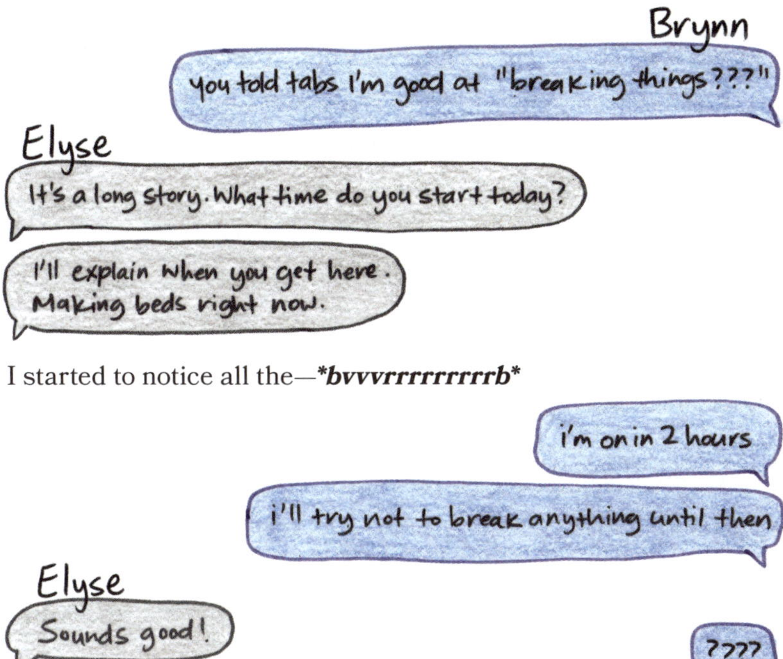

I started to notice all the—***bvvvrrrrrrrrb***

(If I didn't like this job so much, I would burn my notebook and start over somewhere else.)

I started to notice all the labels people freely give themselves at work—usually without being asked any of my pre-approved and not-at-all-inappropriate questions I have prepped and ready in the back of my mind. Labels like:

- Work Wife + Work Husband
- Work BFFs
- The Boss Everyone Flirts With But Wouldn't Actually Hit on For Real Because He's Happily Married But If He's So Happily Married Then Why Is He Flirting Back In The First Place and Why Doesn't He Wear a Wedding Ring?

If I pay close enough attention, I can pinpoint the exact moment someone begins to transform into *The Tour Guide of Them!* Drawing a map of themselves right in front of me.

Likes and dislikes.

Hobbies.

Family trees.

Personal tidbits from their past they enjoy saying out loud.

And a million other small things they don't realize are important to them *but clearly are*, because they're telling someone they just met for the very first time.

Whether it's intentional or not, people tell me who they are by what they share. How they share it. When they share it. How much they share about it. If they seem embarrassed about all their sharing. By being Just The Right Amount of Observant, I've also learned that Tour Guides mention things they *don't* want me asking about at all.

Ever.

No matter what.

In fact, it's my job as the Listener—and the recipient of their Map—to be able to decipher between places that are safe to walk through and places that are way too dangerous, even if they feel Undangerous to me.

The Dangerous Places are only on the Map so I know to avoid them. *Some* people can walk straight through Dangerous Places I Consider Undangerous because they've been equipped by the Tour Guide with the Exact Right Tools and also a little tiny secondary Map that says HOW TO NAVIGATE THROUGH THIS DANGEROUS PLACE! across the top.

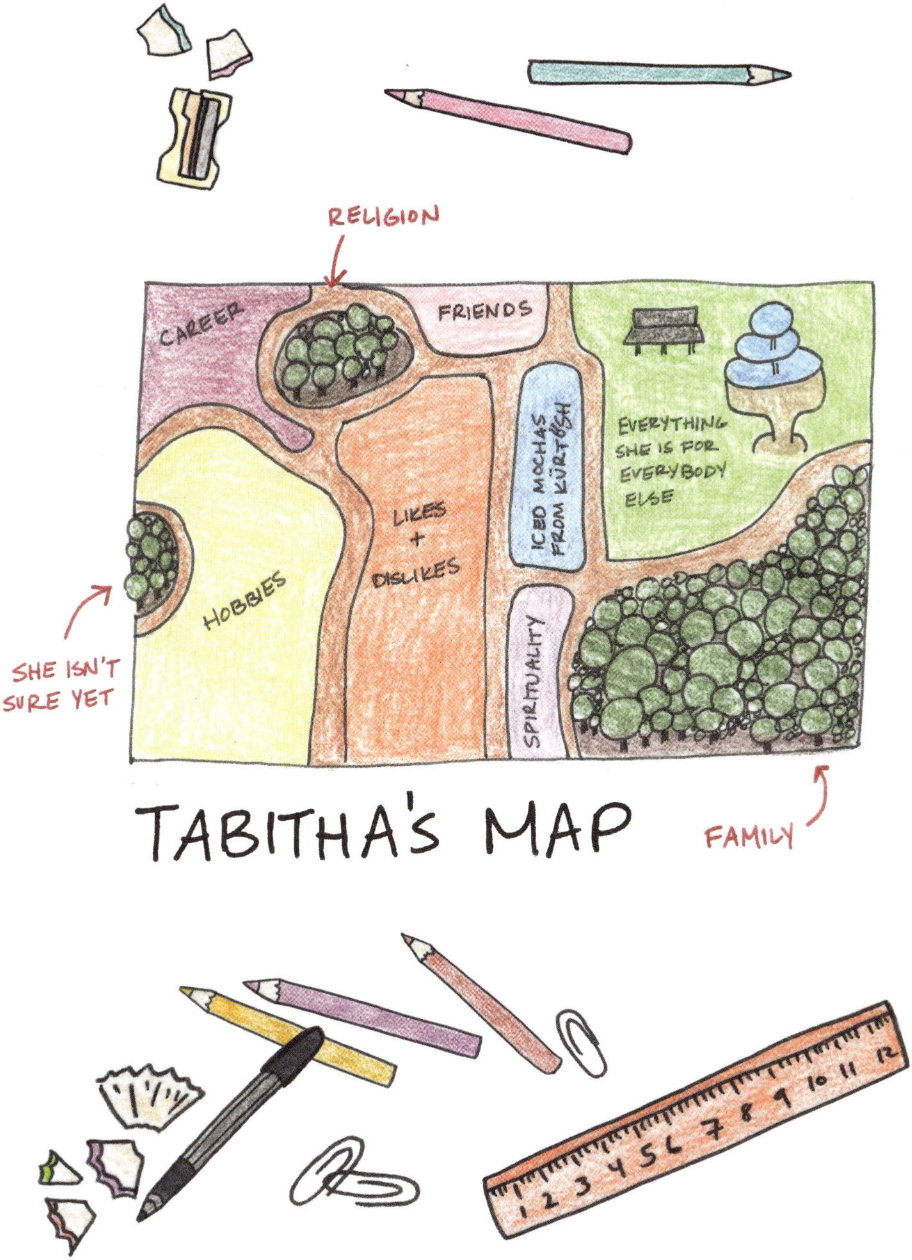

RELIGION

CAREER

FRIENDS

ICED MOCHAS FROM KÜRTŐSH

EVERYTHING SHE IS FOR EVERYBODY ELSE

LIKES + DISLIKES

HOBBIES

SPIRITUALITY

SHE ISN'T SURE YET

TABITHA'S MAP

FAMILY

A place most Listeners are only equipped to avoid, as per the request of the Tour Guide.

There are usually many different Dangerous Places on someone's Map. You'll find all of them if you spend enough time with the Tour Guide. And if you're me, you'll find every single one of them before the Tour has even started.

The part that matters the most—navigating through someone's Dangerous Places I Consider Undangerous—is the very part that makes me realize I wasn't born with the intuitive skills to read people's Maps.

I can *make* Maps—I'm very good at making Maps. I'm also very good at being The Best Listener. Seriously. A Gold Star Listener. Tell me everything about yourself and then tell me even more after that! Let's make a ~~motherfucking~~ MAP! Unfortunately, making the Map is only so helpful. Knowing how to read someone's Map is...well, I don't really know what it is.

Because I can't do it.

HOW TO NAVIGATE THROUGH THIS DANGEROUS PLACE!
SECRET GATE
MOM
DAD
EVERYONE ELSE
(+ ALSO MOM)
(+ ALSO DAD)

How to Fold Hospital Corners in 10 Easy Steps

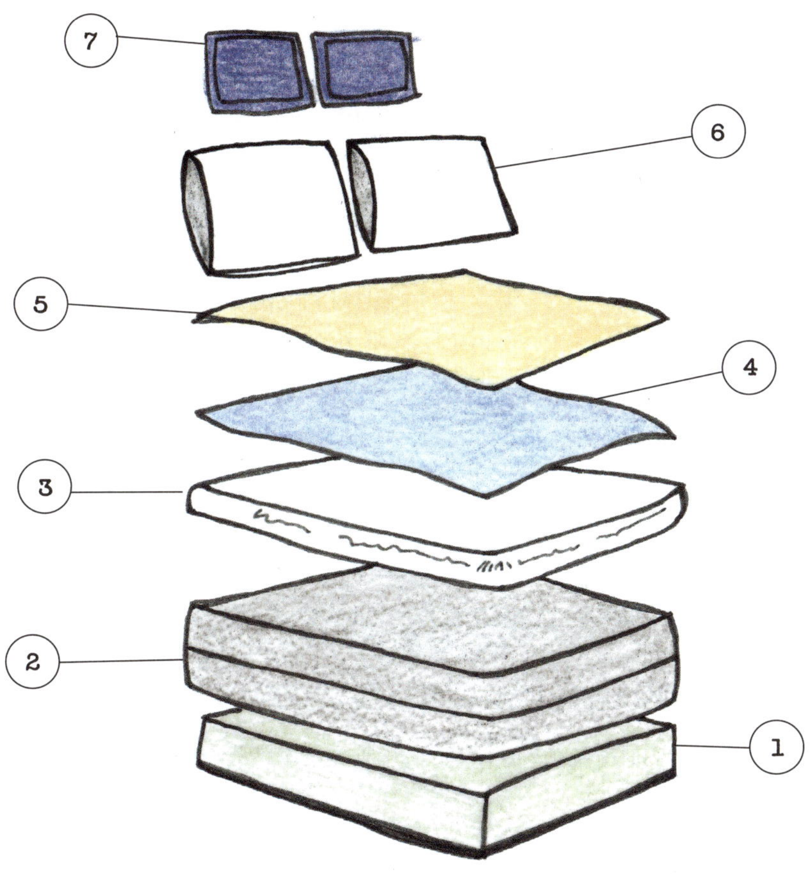

MATERIALS NEEDED:

1. Bed Frame
2. Mattress
3. Fitted Sheet
4. Flat Sheet
5. Duvet
6. Large Pillows
7. Decorative Pillows

STEP ONE: THE FITTED SHEET

1b. If you skip this step, then I don't know what to tell you other than *I think you need to evaluate some of your preferences, because who sleeps without a Fitted Sheet on their bed?* You know what, though? You're probably in the middle of doing laundry and you forgot to put your Fitted Sheet in the dryer so it's drying right now. While you're waiting for it to dry so you can go to sleep, you're probably learning how to make your bed with Hospital Corners because you've always wondered how people do that, so you've finally decided *enough is enough*.

1c. Me, personally? I have some issues with Fitted Sheets, but I'll take those up with Fitted Sheets directly. It would be ridiculous for you to be present when I tell Fitted Sheets that their corners are being made *way* too shallow.

1d. Fitted Sheets always slip off the corner of my bed in the middle of the night when I can't put them back onto the mattress quite the same way as I would if I weren't *in* bed, lying *on top* of the Fitted Sheet. I never remember to fix the corners until I'm lying in bed and the corners slip off in the middle of the night—again—and wake me up from a dream I really didn't want to end. I haven't been dreaming a lot lately and I miss dreaming very much.

1e. Why do the corners always smack you in the face when they pop off the mattress? It feels personal somehow, and I know it isn't but that doesn't mean it doesn't *feel* personal. Just that it *isn't* personal. It would be pointless for you to be present while I told Fitted Sheets all of that. I'll save you the time.

STEP TWO:
THE FLAT SHEET

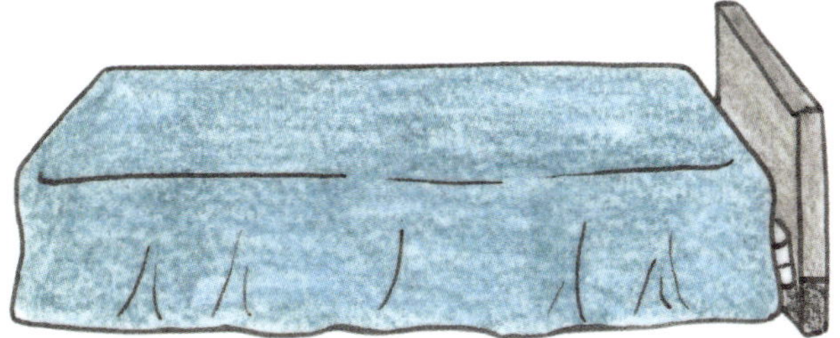

2a. Lay a Flat Sheet on the bed so it hangs evenly over each side. Flat Sheet, Top Sheet, this sheet has many different names. Many—*as in two*—different names. Whatever you call this sheet, the most important thing is you aren't holding the Sheet That Is Impossible to Fold (aka the fitted sheet).

2b. I *really* hate using Top Sheets because I get suspiciously sweaty while I sleep, so the last thing I'm thinking when I'm getting into bed is: *I wish I had one more piece of material draped over me right now!* When I think about it, the irrational dislike that I harbor for Top Sheets makes no sense at all, because I really love using heavy comforters that feel like they're smothering me while I sleep. When I say "smothering," I mean just a tiny bit. Just a little smothering. I like to feel the weight of the Lightly Smothering Comforter while surrounded by a wall of pillows. I keep my bedroom a cool sixty-five degrees, and I sleep with the ceiling fan on high, as well as with a small fan on my nightstand that points directly toward my face all night.

2c. The whole fan situation is something I started as a kid because I needed white noise to be able to fall asleep, but now I feel like I cannot breathe without air being forced into my face by this small but powerful fan. So, yes, I get very sweaty while I sleep. But I guess I can't classify my sleep as Suspiciously Sweaty, can I? With all the light smothering and pillow walls, there's nothing Suspicious about that sweat. Anyway, I avoid the Top Sheet when I can. But when folding Hospital Corners, you'll need it.

STEP THREE:
TUCKING & EXISTENTIAL DREAD

3a. Tuck the sheet in at the foot of the bed but leave the sides untucked. Sweep your hand and tuck it under the mattress so the sheet is really nice and tight. The whole thing about Hospital Corners is that they look impossibly tight, like the bed was wrapped in paper or whatever wrapping it was wrapped in when the mattress was brand new. If you don't get the sheet tight enough, it's basically all a waste.

3b. Not the effort that you put into learning how to fold Hospital Corners—that's not a waste. Energy spent learning something new is never a waste. It's valuable even when the end result isn't what you were hoping for. Didn't Thomas Edison say something like: "*I learned one hundred different ways that light bulbs aren't made?*" I just looked it up and—while the general vibe is the same—the actual quote is pretty different. "*I have not failed, I've just found ten thousand ways that won't work.*" I was also missing two zeroes in my original paraphrase of Edison's quote, which is kind of insulting to him if you think about it, but I'm not going to think about it and neither should you.

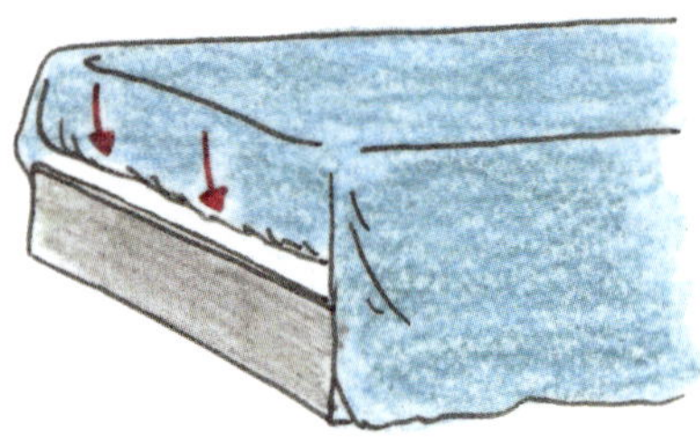

3c. It's kind of wild that the difference between the number 100 and 10,000 is both a *single* number (the number 0, but two of them) and also 9,900 numbers. That's definitely something I could waste some time thinking about. Would you be ashamed of me if I told you that I had to pull my calculator out to double check that 10,000 – 100 = 9,900, just like I thought it was? Imagine how embarrassing it would be to get your math wrong on such a simple equation in a book that will be printed and live forever. Longer than you and I will live! That would be so embarrassing, honestly. *This book is going to outlive me.* ~~I'm suppressing thoughts about how long I might live and the fact that everyone dies at some point.~~

STEP FOUR:
HOW ARE YOU FEELING?

4a. Pick one of the corners at the foot of the bed to start with.

4b. Is your jaw clenched right now? Unclench it.

4c. Relax your shoulders too, while you're at it.

4d. When was the last time you had a glass of water?

STEP FIVE:
LOCATE ALL YOUR RULERS

5a. Hold the sheet about twelve inches from the corner.

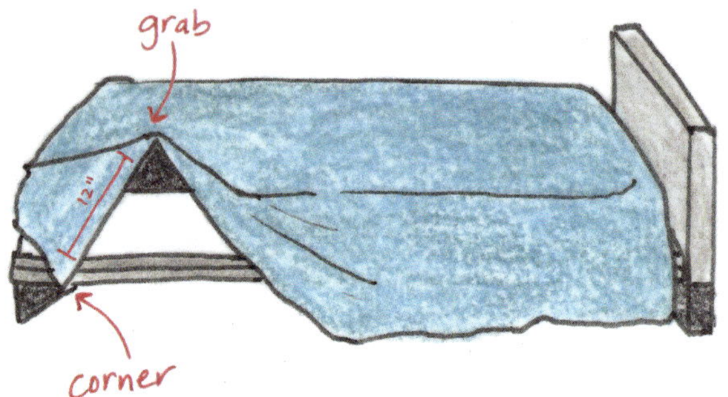

5b. Do you have a ruler? If you don't, you might want to go find one. Not because you actually need it for *this*, but because I can never find my rulers when I need them. You know when I *usually* find all my rulers? When I have absolutely no need for them.

5c. It might be good to locate every ruler you own and decide on a permanent storage spot for them. You should also tell everyone you live with where the rulers live, because when deciding on your rulers' new home, The Deciding is only one part of it. If you don't tell anyone else about the rulers' change of address, then what was all of this *Looking* and *Finding* and *Moving* for anyway?

5d. If you don't tell anyone about the ruler situation, someone might use your ruler and then put it in Any Old Place when they're done! They'll have *no idea* where that ruler lives or that its Temporary Home was replaced with a Forever Home the night its owner decided to learn how to make their bed The Hospital Way.

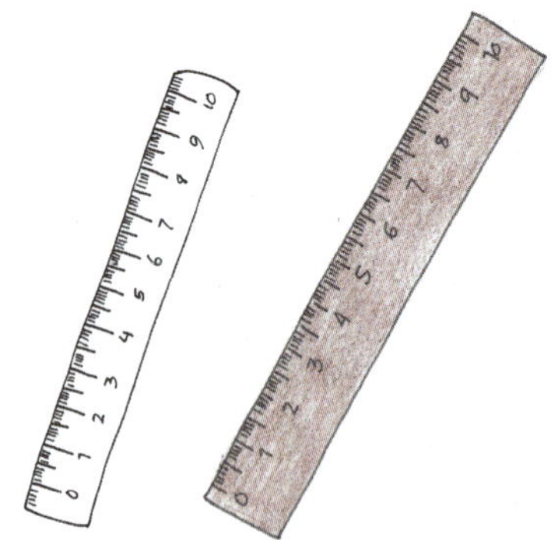

5e. Text your housemates if you have to, because they deserve to know where the rulers live! You owe *them* that, and you *definitely* owe your rulers that! Those rulers rely on you—and whoever you're about to text right now—to return them when they get taken out and used. Imagine getting picked up for dinner and then your date just leaves you at the restaurant because they got The Eating Part out of the way, so there's no point in driving you back home now. You'd find your way home eventually, but it would probably take you a while.

5f. At best, that situation would be very inconvenient for you. At worst? I mean...the worst-case scenario would be Very Very Very Very Very Very Bad. Mostly because you're not a ruler, so the metaphor stops working the moment you start to really break it down.

5g. I find most metaphors work best when they *feel* right, regardless of whether they actually fit the point you're trying to make.

5h. Make sure you really communicate that whole thing (specifically *all of it*) when texting whoever you're texting about the rulers.

5i. I think communication is important. If your rulers could talk, they would say the same thing. But they can't talk because they're rulers and rulers don't talk.*

* If your rulers are talking to you, I think you should tell someone.

STEP SIX:
THE PAPER AIRPLANE FOLD

6a. See the corner of the Top Sheet you're holding in your hand? Lay it on top of the mattress and make a crease at a forty-five-degree angle.

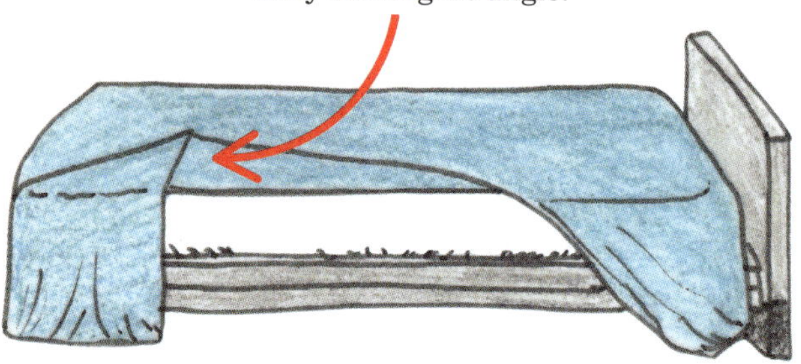

6b. It should resemble the beginning of a Paper Airplane (if you have absolutely no idea how to make Paper Airplanes and you've never actually seen a Paper Airplane in real life). You do *NOT* want to ask me for instructions on how to make Paper Airplanes. I am much better at Hospital Corners than Paper Airplanes. I don't know if I've ever met *anyone* who is as bad at making Paper Airplanes as I am, which might be pretty surprising to anyone who's met me and has said:

> Wow! That's a really cool Paper Airplane tattoo on your arm! What does it mean?

...and then after someone asks me that question, I get a little weird and quiet because it's kind of a long story. But it's not sad! Usually long stories are sad. This is not that kind of story. I mean, the story isn't completely happy. There are definitely some parts in there—especially at the beginning—that might make you go "that's kind of a bummer" but that's just the beginning. You have to keep listening for it all to make sense.

6c. That's the whole point of a story, isn't it? That there's a beginning, and then there's also the entire rest of it? I don't think I would categorize the story of my Paper Airplane Tattoo as anything but Very Good and Won't Make You Sad After You Hear It. I might ask you how much time you have before I start telling The Story, to which you might reply:

> I actually don't have very much time. I just saw your tattoo and thought it was really cool so I asked about it but now I realize I have to be somewhere else.

6d. It doesn't seem to matter how many times I've changed my Paper Airplane technique; they like to nosedive every single time. You should ask my brother Kyle to teach you how to make Paper Airplanes. Kyle makes the best Paper Airplanes. He used to stand at the top of my grandma's staircase and throw his Paper Airplanes off the top step and—I swear—one flew out the front door and landed perfectly on the lawn of my neighbor across the street. You should ask him about it sometime!

6e. He won't tell you about the carpet at my grandma's house, which was the most curious shade of marigold my eyeballs have ever seen.

6f. Kyle didn't appreciate the carpet like I did. The color of the carpet made spills completely undetectable. I'm serious. Do you know how much cereal milk I've spilled on that carpet? I never considered until right this very minute that all my spilled cereal milk must have dried and smelled terrible. That had to have happened eventually, right?

6g. My grandma doesn't live in the house with marigold carpet anymore, but Kyle still makes very good Paper Airplanes.

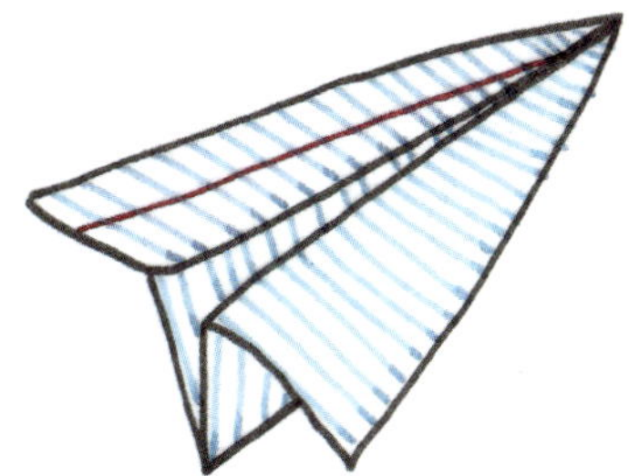

STEP SEVEN:
FAKE IT 'TIL YOU MAKE IT

7a. Tuck the excess sheet under the mattress with your free hand. Tuck it *tightly* so you get clean lines. I'm not kidding when I said this is all a waste if those lines aren't clean and if the sheet isn't tight.

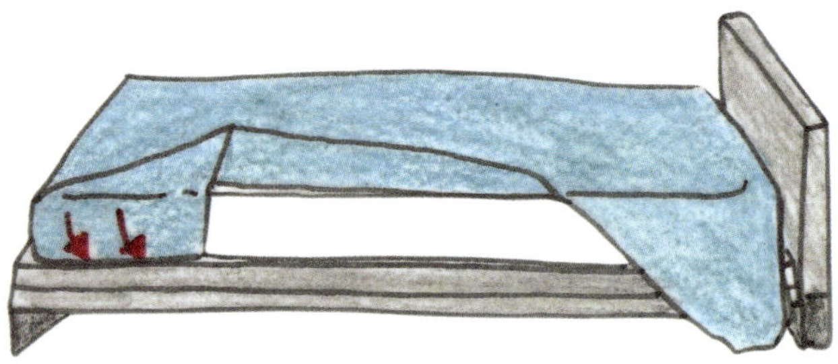

7b. When someone walks past your bed, do you want them to think, *That is a very regular and normal bed?* OR! Do you want them to think, *If this person has the time to fold Hospital Corners, they MUST have their life together and absolutely nothing is wrong at all!*

7c. I don't have my life together right now, but maybe I can trick myself into thinking I do if my bed looks like Someone Whose Life Is Fully Together. I am a big fan of Fake It 'Til You Make It—so much so that sometimes I lie to myself and then I believe my own lies and then forget I was ever sad in the first place!

7d. This is not healthy and I know that, but something being Healthy and something being Effective are two completely different things.

7e. Sometimes a person (me) just needs something to work so they (I) can hang on until it's time to crawl back into bed and enjoy their (my) tightly tucked Hospital Corners that give the perception that: Everything Is Totally And Completely Fine, Nothing Is Wrong, and Everything Is Going To Be Okay!

STEP EIGHT:
EVERYTHING IS GOING TO BE OKAY

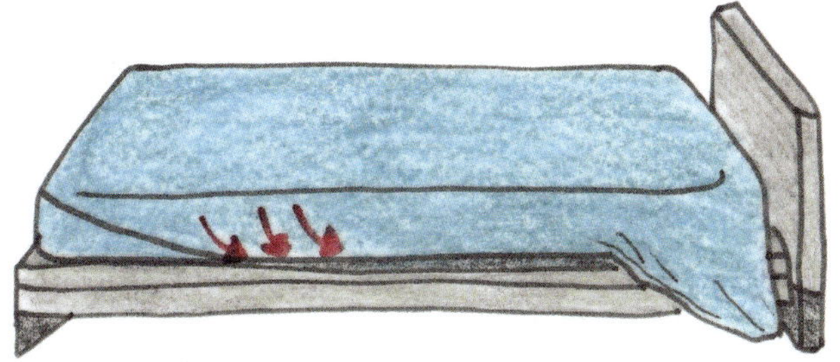

8a. Tuck the Paper Airplane piece under the mattress.

8b. Everything really is going to be Okay. That isn't a lie. Sometimes things don't feel like they're going to be anything except for Not Okay. Sometimes days feel long—so much longer than days used to feel. The Very Long Days end up passing, and eventually Days That Didn't Feel Long Enough To Be A Day At All end up passing too.

8c. At some point, you might even find yourself saying, *Hey! This is a day! The Short Kind!* But everything becoming Okay happens slowly. I don't usually notice when I first start Feeling Better, and I can't pinpoint the exact moment I feel So Much Better that I barely remember feeling anything *except* So Much Better.

8d. As many times as Unfoldable Fitted Sheets need to be washed so they can get back to slipping off mattress corners, and as many times as Top Sheets get creased like poorly constructed Paper Airplanes, and mattresses get stripped and redressed, and rulers get moved, and cereal milk gets hidden in marigold carpet—*that* is as many times as you might feel yourself slide between Not Okay and So Much Better.

STEP NINE:
I'M REALLY SORRY I WALKED IN ON YOU HAVING SEX

9a. Tuck any excess sheet tightly underneath the mattress.

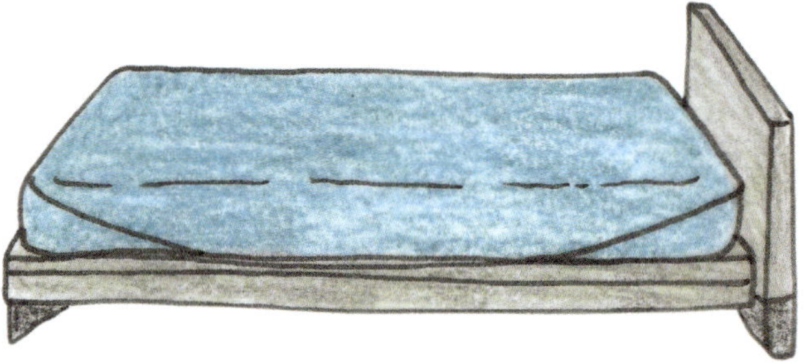

9b. I cannot stress enough how important the tightness of your sheet is to the success of this whole thing. Everything should look sterile—as though no one has ever used the bed you're about to sleep in, even though your bed has been used very much! It has been used so many times! In so many different ways! And if you're folding Hospital Corners in a hotel room like I just did before I sat down to write this, those beds have been used in more ways than I ever wanted to know beds could be used!

9c. Hotel beds are used in ways I don't think are super appropriate to mention right now, given the fact that this is a list of instructions.

9d. They're used in ways that make me regret accidentally walking in on when performing a mandatory wellness check for a guest that hadn't left their hotel room in three days. As it turned out, he was completely fine and aggressively unclothed with a stranger they met in the hotel lobby so they couldn't hear me calling their phone or the loud knocks at their door!

9e. But that's the beauty of Hospital Corners! They help you forget! This bed is brand-new, and the folds in the sheet are so crispy and the tucks are so perfectly tight that the memory of anyone existing in this bed before you has been tightly tucked right out of it!

STEP TEN:
THIS STEP DOESN'T EXIST

There is no step number ten.

But letting a list of instructions end at step number nine would be absurd.

(If you give yourself a little more time, Not Okay might turn into So Much Better without you realizing it's even happening.)

Everything She's Ever Wanted

(to say but only remembers when she's angry and taking a shower)

"...all that to say, I love you. I'm *in love* with you."

Silence, and so much of it.

"Are you still there?"

"Hmm?"

"Just making sure you heard me."

"Which part?" She heard him. Of course she heard him. She's incapable of not hearing him. He's made himself such a large part of her life that she couldn't *not hear him* if she tried.

And she's tried so many times, each time less successful than the last.

"All of it? I'm sorry if I said too much. Can you at least say...something? Anything?"

"I heard everything, but..." If she wasn't already sitting on the floor of her closet, she would have found the nearest Sittable Surface and planted herself there. "Can you just...I mean, I can't, um...If you could give me a second or two?"

His shallow breath is the last thing she hears before she drops the phone into her lap and presses the heels of her palms against her eyes. She wants everything to stop being so *much* for just one second so she can try to remember everything he said tonight. Everything she has been waiting years to hear him say.

There was a day when hearing him tell her how much he loves

her wouldn't have completely broken her heart, like it's breaking right this very second. When it wasn't too late, and it wasn't because he was about to lose her to someone else if he didn't.

But that day came and went, and many more days came and went after that.

Her phone is burning a hole in her lap, and she can feel the rest of her heart breaking, his words finishing the job he started so many years ago. She lets herself have sixty seconds of complete and total silence at the bottom of her closet, then pulls the phone up to her ear.

She used to imagine what it would feel like to finally hear him say it. She had dreams so vivid they would wake her up. They felt *nothing* like this. Because when she imagined getting Everything She's Ever Wanted, she didn't anticipate being crushed by its weight.

Tonight feels nothing like the dreams that used to wake her up or the moments she imagined while trying to fall back asleep. With the remaining few seconds, she finds all the words she was too afraid to say *last* time she got Everything She's Ever Wanted. She was silly and assumed the next time it came around, it would really be *Everything* She's Ever Wanted.

"You don't love me. You're just scared of losing me," she says.

"That's not what's happening here, and you know it." His voice seems loud and sharp and angry and many other things she never imagined hearing in his voice when he told her he loved her.

"Is it not?" Her eyes are burning with unshed tears and her throat is on fire. She doesn't want to give him the satisfaction of crying, so she finds more room in her chest to store all the emotion she's waiting to release until after she hangs up the phone.

She continues: "You only tell me you love me when I can't say it back. Why does it take me finding someone that is kind and nice and treats me well, and makes me *happy*, for you to tell me that you love me? I'm not a game you get to play when you're bored and lonely, or when you want someone to make you feel important. You don't get to keep ruining my life because you're afraid I might not be in yours one day."

"I'm a mess! Is that what you want to hear? That I'm a mess? You have *always* deserved more than I could give you. I know you don't believe me, but that's the truth. You deserve someone who is as *good* as you believe they are. But I want to try! I'm ready to try! I *want* to be the good person you think I am!" He pushes the last of his words out before his throat sounds too thick with emotion to say anything else. She can hear his voice shake on the other end of the line as he begins to cry.

"I don't think you have a goddamn clue what you're ready for. But what I do know is that you're a coward." Her voice hitches in the back of her throat, and she is dangerously close to crying. She's never been good at being honest without Tears volunteering themselves as Honesty's automatic companion. "Do you want to know the worst part about losing everything I've ever wanted? *Twice?*"

He remains silent, unsure of whether her question is rhetorical or not.

"*Do you?!* Because I would *love* to tell you! The worst part about losing everything I've ever wanted is that I can't even pretend I don't know what it feels like to have it. To have you. You told me you loved me once and then you disappeared. You looked me in the eyes. *Finally* told me you loved me. And then I didn't see you or hear from you for a *year*!" She hates how loud her voice has become, and she hates even more that he gets to hear how hurt she still is. She takes a deep breath and shifts her body so she's sitting up a little taller than before.

This is the last time she will ever speak to him.

She refuses to let the grief in her heart clobber the resolve in her mind.

She continues: "I spent months crawling my way out of the hole you buried me in. I've *finally* started to let you go, and you can't stand it! You don't *want* me! But now, you don't want to *lose* me! For a second time, you have stolen the microscopic amount of mercy that exists in *not knowing* what it feels like to hear you tell me you love me. And you don't even mean it. *That's* the worst part about losing everything I've ever wanted...it was taken from me by the same coward that should never have given it to me in the first place."

He takes an exaggerated breath, and she can already hear his beautifully crafted excuse forming even before he starts speaking. "I didn't know I was—"

"*Oh god, ohhhmygod!* Oh...Damn it!"
She throws her face into the stream of water and watches the suds from her shampoo circle the drain.
She drags the scent of her vanilla conditioner through her wet hair.

That would have been so good *too!* she thinks.
The worst part about LOSING everything I've ever wanted?
Why can't I ever say things like that when it matters?!

She closes her eyes and lets the warm water run down her back.
She feels herself once again drifting into her head...

"You made a decision for me that wasn't yours to make. You're so afraid of not being enough that you'd rather run as far away from me as you can and break my heart before I ever have the chance to break yours. I think you believe you love me, but I'm certain that you don't. Because if you really loved me like you think you do, you would have learned how to say it without one foot already out the door, and before I finally let myself learn how to love somebody that isn't you."

She can no longer hold back the tears that have been pooling in her eyes since she first picked up the phone and heard his voice.

"Love doesn't feel like this, and I will never let you make me feel like *this* ever again. I want to be loved by someone who knows how to stay and knows how to love me all the time. So please, if you care about me at all, as much as you say you do, never tell me you love me again. I am *begging* you to let me let you go."

A silence falls over the line that feels so dense it might choke them both.

"Okay," he finally says.

"Okay," she replies.

"Can I ask you one more question?"

"No." Her voice is sharp. She's never sounded as unfamiliar to him as she does right now.

"Are you happy?" he asks anyway.

After a long pause, she says, "Yes." She's lying.

"Are you sure?" He already knows the answer to this question because she's a terrible liar.

"Yes." She lies again, this time to herself.

"Okay."

"Okay."

So many things she could have said.

And she said "*okay*."

...all that to say, I love you. I'm *in love* with you.

[silence]

Are you still there?

Hmm?

Just making sure you heard me.

Which part?

All of it? I'm sorry if I said too much.

I heard everything.
Can you just—I can't, um...I can't think. I just need a second.

[a suffocating amount of silent seconds]

I can't.

Okay.

Okay.

Are you happy?

Yes.

Are you sure?

Yes.

Okay.

Okay.

House Clothes

I knew it was coming. We both saw it coming for weeks. And still, I'm sitting here wondering how on earth I wasn't able to make a nearly perfect relationship work with a fully perfect person.

"How do you feel about your newfound singleness?" Alexis asks me while she blows away the steam floating above her bowl of scalding-hot oatmeal. I'm convinced she has no feeling in her mouth at all, because the contents of the bowl she's about to eat are surely boiling.

Or whatever the equivalent of boiling is when talking about oatmeal and not water.

Simmering?

No, boiling.

It has to be boiling.

I am watching it boil.

I wonder if the high pain tolerance is a Brazilian thing or just an Alexis thing.

"You feel good? Or no?"

Do I feel good about my Newfound Singleness? Ahhhh, yes. The singleness I newly found somewhere over the Pacific Ocean and inside invisible Wi-Fi signals, in between two computer screens that know each other very well and during three different video calls—all lasting somewhere around thirty minutes and three hours. Video calls that always ended with deconstructing where our relationship went wrong and why neither of us was to blame for our lowercase (love) that I'd hoped would turn into The Uppercase Kind of *LOVE!* if we just gave it more time and also more of every other flavor of More two people might try to feed their (love).

Because that's what people do when they hope their (love) will grow into *LOVE!*

We asked for—and tried to give each other—many different kinds of More. But by the end, there wasn't any More to be found. Instead, I found Singleness in More's place.

I watch as Alexis dollops peanut butter and Nutella onto her boiling oats. She makes the same breakfast every single day, and every day I think, *I should really try that. It looks delicious.* But this morning I'm not thinking about how delicious peanut butter and Nutella taste when they're mixed into oatmeal that was once boiling but has had time to cool off and is still boiling.

I'm distracted by the way Alexis just described the death of my relationship with my long-distance boyfriend who was perfect in every way. Except that he just wasn't perfect for *me*.

Newfound Singleness.

It sounds so magical when worded that way, doesn't it? Not at all sad or disappointing.

Definitely not like a gigantic bummer.

"Newfound Singleness" doesn't even sound like a breakup. It sounds like a surprise gift card you find in the pocket of your old jeans that's worth an obscure amount of money and can't actually buy you anything without also having to spend your own money too, but at least it's something!

Or when you read your work schedule wrong and walk into the back office to clock in and your boss asks you what you're doing there and you say, "I'm working," and they say, "No, you aren't," and then you say, "No, you're so right, I'm not," because you did, in fact, read the schedule wrong and as a result you have an entire day to spend however you choose. But you're in your work uniform and all your friends are working so you'd kind of rather just be working, but it's still a day off so you get ice cream and try to make the most of all this accidental free time.

It's the addition of something unexpected.

It doesn't sound like a loss at all.

There are so many things Newfound Singleness *sounds* like, and none of them sounds the way being newly single feels: sad. (*Mostly* sad, with a few self-indulgent thoughts of all these feelings being equal parts temporary and never-ending and absolutely necessary and sometimes seasoned with a little bit of "Maybe I'll die alone because I've reached the elderly age of twenty-two and my best years are behind me, which means I'm definitely never going to fall in love ever again.")

I watch Alexis spoon large bites of peanut butter and chocolate oatmeal into her steel mouth and am aware that I need to get out of the house.

"I'm getting out of the house."

I haven't spoken much since I woke up this morning, so my voice sounds dry and scratchy and a little bit pathetic.

"Good!" Alexis says, spooning away at her oatmeal.

"Good." I grab my backpack off my bedroom floor and leave.

Alexis calls out behind me after the door is already closed: "You're still wearing your pajamas!"

I don't bother going back into the apartment. I yell back, *"They're not pajamas, they're house clothes!"* because I know she'll be able to hear me through our front door, which has slowly been falling apart. I can't believe it hasn't fully disintegrated into a fine dust or fallen off the hinges, given how many times a day it gets slammed shut by the six of us who live behind it.

While I'm waiting for the elevator to pick me up from the fifteenth floor and take me down to the lobby, Alexis peeks her head out into the hallway.

"If they're house clothes, then why are you wearing them outside?"

"Why are you whispering?" I whisper back, unintentionally matching the volume of her voice.

"Why are you *shouting*?" she whisper-shouts back.

I'm starting to feel the weight of what it means to live with five other roommates who all come from different parts of the world. Our apartment represents six countries and four different continents.

Brazil.

Indonesia.

Canada.

New Zealand.

United States.

Philippines.

Surprisingly, no one is from Australia.

Most of the fights that happen in our apartment are a result of some deep cultural offense that we aren't aware we've committed until the argument has already started and more than one person is crying out of sympathy. It's like you're playing dodgeball blindfolded, but no one told you that you were playing dodgeball or why you're blindfolded, and also you've never heard of dodgeball in your life.

"House clothes are basically like normal clothes. They're

just...a little more comfy. Like what you'd wear while watching a movie! I just *call* them house clothes, but you can leave the house in them—"

"Those are pajamas."

Wait. This isn't a culture thing, this is just a preference thing.

A familiar bell rings as I hear the elevator door open behind me. I am still staring at Alexis, watching her try to make sense of the fact that I would willingly leave our apartment in any type of clothing she considers pajamas. I watch her eyes run over my body, starting at my frizzy hair and ending at my sandals, which are falling apart. Technically they fell apart about a year ago, but duct tape has been keeping them together until I can buy a new pair when I move back to the States in a few months.

"Beleza, tchau."

Alexis's head slithers out from the space between the door and its frame, as she returns inside to her oatmeal. The door slams shut. I love Alexis.

I also feel like Alexis could kill me with her eyeballs if she stared at me long enough.

"What's with the pajamas?"

Aiden is standing in the doorway of the foyer that extends underneath our classrooms. The large glass doors are propped open, and the sound of students talking over one another bounces and echoes through the tiled interior of the building and floods out the front door. There can't be more than thirty students standing in the foyer behind Aiden, but the wall of noise makes those thirty voices sound like three hundred.

"They aren't pajamas, they're *house clothes*."

"This is kind of a weird day to wear house clothes, isn't it?"

"What are you talking ab—oh shit. OH SHIT. Aiden, I forgot today was *today*!"

Aiden and I are in charge of leading tonight's rehearsal for the end-of-semester Songwriter Showcase that's taking place at the main college campus, which is an hour away by bus (if we leave at exactly the right time and hit zero traffic). When I look down to assess how urgent my clothing situation is, I realize I might have no other choice than to be late.

(Again.)

"Of course I'm wearing pajamas today. Of course!"

"I thought you said they weren't pajamas?"

I'm pulling at my hair out of nervous habit.

I picture holding a microphone in my hand and directing well-respected songwriters, singers, and musicians from the front of a large room while wearing ancient, semi-transparent soccer shorts with disintegrated elastic at the waist that need to be held up by a hair tie to protect me from getting pantsed by gravity in public.

Technically, I can find a way to make these shorts work.

I have in the past.

But the Looney Tunes graphic t-shirt that's three sizes too big—and is *so* wrinkled it looks like a piece of paper that was dug out of the trash—really shoves me over the cliff of indecision. I have to run back to my apartment to get a change of clothes.

Someone makes a loud announcement that the buses will be leaving in ten minutes. I can make it back to my apartment in four if I sprint as fast as I can and I don't get caught waiting at the one stoplight we have between campus and my apartment building.

Aiden is watching my face as I do the mental math, calculating whether I can actually make it back in time to be on the bus when it leaves with all thirty songwriting students plus Aiden. With as much softness as he can inject into his consistent and brutal honesty, Aiden says:

"You look like garbage. It's worth running back."

"GREAT, THANKS, I'LL BE RIGHT BACK."

I drop my backpack at Aiden's feet and begin sprinting as fast as I can. I'm not sure what it is about these band rehearsals, but I'm never late to *anything* and I have been late to every single one of them.

I run past the empty building that used to be a café where I worked as a barista the first summer I lived in Sydney. I stopped working there because the café owners were arrested for taking on fake identities to get out of paying taxes from the last café they opened. I met them as Rachel and Thalad, and when Thalad introduced himself to me, I said: "Like 'salad' with a lisp?"

And he: didn't laugh.

And I: felt bad for a while, but now that I know Thalad wasn't even his real name, I don't feel so bad about it anymore. In fact, I'm a little upset that he didn't laugh, because it was a quality joke. Maybe inappropriate because he was my boss, but *definitely* funny. I never received a single paycheck the entire summer I worked at that café, which makes me significantly more upset than Thalad not laughing at my joke, but not so significantly that I won't bring up both memories in tandem. Even though I never got paid, I *did* learn how to make a beautiful latte, and in Australia, that's basically better than a paycheck! (It definitely isn't, but I tell myself it is so I don't spiral.)

I run past a person holding a glass bottle of organic almond milk.

The duct tape on one of my sandals breaks, so I take off both of my sandals and keep running.

I sprint past another café, which I'd stopped working at about six months earlier. The owners of this café were fully real and their identities not fake at all!

Which is great!

Unless you take into account the whole "getting locked in a supply closet because one of the managers didn't appreciate my turning down his many sexual advances so he finally said, 'Enough is enough!' and his solution was to lock the handle of the supply closet door from the outside while I was getting more napkins and coffee cup sleeves and told me to 'think about what I want out of life' in the hope my answer would be 'You! Overwhelmingly!' but he didn't consider that the closet door had a safety doorknob that could be unlocked if you put your fingernail into the little groove in the back in the event that this *exact* emergency should ever take place" thing.

If you don't take *that* into account, then it was a pretty great job!

He was fired, and I quit. I have a weird thing about supply closets now.

I hate them.

I sprint past *another* café, one where I'm a regular at now, because the café I just broke up with is fine, but I got tired of how warm it gets because they like to open the windows instead of turn on the air conditioner, and so now every time I go inside I feel bad that I haven't been in a while and it's kind of like seeing an ex-boyfrie—oh.

I forgot.

For a brief moment, I forgot.

I am running and I feel bile rising in the base of my throat, and I am running and I am barefoot and I forgot all about my Newfound Singleness.

I can see the top of my apartment building poking above the trees, and I am still running.

Straight through the dog park.

Past the weird fountain that isn't a fountain.

Past the public pool and shared gym that belongs to all the residents of the apartment complex clump I live in.

Past the dumpsters in the parking lot that gave me my perfectly good nightstand.

I forgot.

I can't tell if I'm feeling misplaced adrenaline because I'm running as fast as I can and I'm not a runner so my body thinks I'm gearing up to fight a bear, or if I'm just feeling myself slowly being pulled under by the Rip Current of Remembering.

It's both.

It's definitely both.

But I am single and I am still running and I can see the front doors to the lobby of my apartment building and I am still running and I am as close to my apartment building as I am to throwing up and I am still running.

It took me three minutes to run here.

I have never run this fast in my life.

I think I'd like to keep running, but I don't have time.

The elevator takes me up to the fifteenth floor, and I run through the front door of my apartment, not acknowledging Alexis sitting on the couch in the living room in jeans.

The door slams behind me.

Jeans on a couch in your free time feels egregious, but these are the exact feelings that earned me a three-minute sprint, six minutes round trip, to my apartment. If I was more like Alexis and wore jeans while lounging on a couch, I wouldn't be in this position right now.

I grab the first clean shirt I see and the only pair of jeans I own and leave as quickly and as loudly as I came in.

The door slams behind me.

I make it to the bus on time. I don't even throw up.

After a very long and sweaty bus ride, I make it to rehearsal on time. Aiden seems pleased with the clothes I shoved into a plastic trash bag and changed into once we got off the bus. I still haven't cooled down since I stopped running. At this rate, I don't think I will. I can already feel the sweat from my back soaking my fresh t-shirt. Once I start sweating, I can't stop.

But my jeans don't require a hair tie to hold them up and I'm not worried about gravity's effect on my pants, and my shirt doesn't have cartoon characters on it.

Altogether, my decision to change clothes has been a Net Positive.

"Why are you walking like that?" Aiden's face tells me the question isn't coming from a place of concern. Aiden is a runner. He runs in his free time. For fun. He tells me often that I might enjoy the "mental and emotional benefits of a runner's high." I don't want to give him the satisfaction of proving him right.

Because I know he's right.

"My legs are sore. Don't worry about it."

"You ran for, like, six minutes."

"They were six very explosive minutes!"

"...All right." If we weren't crunched for time, I know his response would have been doused in sarcasm and just funny enough to not hurt my feelings.

I begin arranging chairs and music stands and microphone packs, making sure everyone has what they need before we begin rehearsing for the end-of-semester Songwriter Showcase. As I'm on the floor digging through my backpack for my notebook, I hear a familiar voice cut through the very long auditorium. It's at least an octave lower than any other voice in the room.

"Why the hell don't you have any dividers!" I whisper into my backpack. "You're a gigantic bucket with a couple of straps, and you eat all my things and never give them back. Where is my notebook? Give me back my notebook!"

The volume of my voice has graduated from a whisper to the Standard Volume At Which Outside Conversations Are Had. (If one human being was speaking to another human being, this would be the exact right way to describe the volume of my voice. But considering I am still speaking to my backpack, it feels pretty loud.)

"Long time no see."

The deep voice is much closer now, almost as if it's speaking directly to—

"Oh my god." I am crouched down on the floor, shoulder-deep in my divider-less black hole of a backpack, and Jonas From The Meat Counter is standing above me.

"You're...here? Why are you...how did—why are you here?"

The last time I saw Jonas, I'd been holding roast beef and cashews and running (figuratively) late (but just barely) to rehearsal for last semester's Songwriter Showcase.

What is it about these rehearsals?

"I don't mean, like, not that I don't *want* you to be here. I just, like—"

"I'm not really here. I work small odds and ends jobs on campus after hours and on the weekends. I was walking through the foyer and saw things getting set up in here. I peeked in to see what was happening and saw some people I knew. And then I saw you. So...now I'm saying hi."

I say nothing. My legs are sore. My back is dripping with sweat. I have lost my notebook in the black hole that lives inside of my backpack. I am drowning in all this Newfound Singleness. I can feel the start of a foot cramp brewing in the arch of my left foot because I refused to buy new sandals and wear clothes that look like clothes you leave your house in.

My mouth tastes like pennies.

And...now I'm talking to Jonas From The Meat Counter with a nice voice and an even nicer beard that I don't remember him having five months ago when I saw him last. I don't remember much about that encounter other than being hungry and also confused about his Hot Takes regarding what makes pasta salad special.

And that he was wearing house clothes to the grocery store just like I do.

I wonder if he calls them house clothes too.

"This is just a quick hello and goodbye. Sorry, I didn't mean to take you out of the zone."

I'm trying to think of something clever to say.

All that ends up leaving my mouth is "Look at this beard!"

I watch my hand reach out and touch Jonas's face.

I'm almost positive I didn't tell my hand to do this.

Surely I am watching someone else's hand do this. Because *my* hand belongs down at my side. Or in my backpack. Or shoved in the front pocket of my jeans (a pocket that is way too small to fit a human hand). But definitely—*definitely*—not touching someone's face.

As if my thumb has a mind of its own, it begins stroking Jonas's cheek. I watch my thumb move back and forth. Back and for—

I rip my hand away. I'm mortified.

"It *is* a beard. Yes," Jonas says, words dripping with surprise. He looks at me like he wants to continue speaking, but is too stunned by the sudden and unexpected physical contact to say anything else.

What the hell was that, Elyse?

"Single for, what, twenty-four hours and already touching people's faces?"

Aiden is standing next to me, and I have no idea how long he's been standing there.

My legs suddenly feel just fine, and I'd like to run away now.

Jonas looks at Aiden.

Then, Jonas looks at me.

Then...Jonas *looks* at me.

I didn't know I liked beards.

Now I know. Without a shadow of a doubt, I like beards.

At least, I like *beard*.

One beard.

One beard on one very specific person.

I would likc to touch it again.

Unfortunately, I believe this interaction is limited to a maximum of one Accidental and/or On-Purpose-Without-Thinking-It-Through Beard Touch per lifetime. Now that I'm fresh out of Beard Touches, I'm going to have to settle for a Violently Apologetic Head Nod and multiple "I'm Sorrys" in a row.

Those are the official rules, I think. I'm not even making them up. I'm pretty sure they're published in a book somewhere, I promise!

"I am...so sorry? I don't even know why I just did that. I'm sorry."

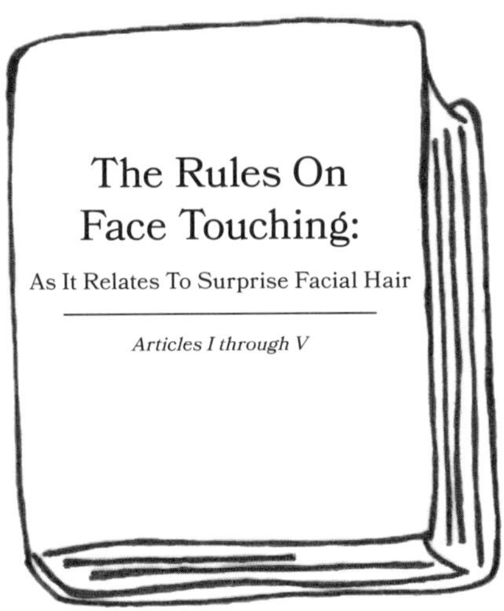

"You don't need to be sorry."

Jonas responds so quickly that I almost don't register it at all.

"I enjoyed it. I don't want you to be sorry."

Jonas takes my hand and brings it back to his face.

"Here." He gently holds his hand over mine as my hand holds hands with his beard.

This act feels painfully intimate. I'm more aware now of the people standing around us and the rehearsal that is officially starting late and my legs that feel sore again and the foot cramp that is no longer brewing but is all the way here, and I'm still touching Jonas's beard.

For a second time.

I pull my hand away from his face—again—as if the feel of his beard under my palm is offensive to me. I begin planning my very casual and very inconspicuous escape from this conversation so that I can hear my own thoughts again and decide whether I need to cry about this later and also right now.

"Well, this has been great, and I like your shirt. Goodbye!" I pivot on my un-cramped foot and feel the carpet beneath me try its best to trip me and force me onto the ground. In an effort to avoid falling, I take one large step, and my leg catches my weight before my face kisses the floor. At this point, I have nothing to lose, because my dignity disappeared the moment I put my Looney Tunes shirt on this morning. I take another, equally large step forward to disguise the fact that I almost just ate the floor, and before I know it, I am running.

I don't think I *meant* to start running, but...I am running.

There's no doubt: I am running away.

If this is going to keep happening, maybe I should start running on purpose.

I'd like to be prepared next time.

The Rules on Face Touching: As It Relates to Surprise Facial Hair

Article I: Limitations on Beard Contact

1. Person(s) are hereby restricted to one (1) Beard Touch [*Accidental and/or On Purpose Without Thinking It Through*] per lifetime. This Beard Touch, having been redeemed, is to be considered nonredeemable and may not be transferred or delegated to any other individual or future interaction. The aforementioned Beard Touch, once executed by the Offending Person(s) [hereby and furthermore referred to as **"Facial Hair Enthusiast"**], is final.
2. Should **Facial Hair Enthusiast** previously specified in **Item 1** redeem their one (1) Beard Touch, **Facial Hair Enthusiast** must strictly follow the apology protocols specifically outlined in Article II, directed solely and immediately to the Offended Person(s) [hereby and furthermore referred to as **"The Bearded One"**].

Article II: The Apology

For the purposes of this contract, **The Apology** shall refer to the obligatory and repetitive expression of regret issued by **Facial Hair Enthusiast** upon the occurrence of an unauthorized facial hair contact. This mandatory verbal statement is intended to mitigate the overwhelming and painful discomfort generated by such an event and reduce, though not eliminate, the inevitable embarrassment that will continue to burden **Facial Hair Enthusiast** for the remainder of their natural life.

The Apology must:

1. Be issued immediately and without hesitation following the realization of the infraction, as any delay will only intensify the level of social discomfort for all parties involved.
2. Be delivered with an appropriate display of sincerity and self-condemnation, ideally signaled by a combination of physical distress (e.g., head nodding) and excessive/unnecessary justification. The physical distress must be executed with sufficient vigor to ensure **The Bearded One** understands the perceived severity of the offense, regardless of their true feelings about the incident at the time it occurred.
3. Contain the four (4) essential words: **"I," "Am," "So,"** and **"Sorry."** The precise order of these words is not material to the validity of **The Apology**; however, the inclusion of all four (4) words is mandatory, and failure to incorporate each word shall render **The Apology** null and void.
4. Be delivered with overzealous explanation and excessive justification, ensuring that the depth of regret is conveyed not only through the words themselves but also through the tone and length of the explanation, even if this results in heightened discomfort for **The Bearded One**.

Failure to properly execute **The Apology** may result in, but is not limited to, the following penalties:

1. An immediate and irrevocable loss of social dignity.
2. Prolonged overanalysis of the event in the form of sleepless nights and sudden pangs of emotional discomfort during otherwise peaceful moments.
3. Persistent nausea and deep personal shame whenever the incident resurfaces in memory.

Article III: Rights of The Bearded One

The Bearded One reserves the right to express confusion, amusement, or mild indignation. However, forgiveness shall be granted by **The Bearded One**, assuming full compliance with **Article II.**

Article IV: Post-Contact Protocol

Following the redemption of the one (1) Beard Touch, **Facial Hair Enthusiast** is legally prohibited from initiating further physical contact with the facial hair in question. Any future engagement with said facial hair must be limited to verbal admiration or visual appreciation from a socially acceptable distance.

Article V: Exceptions and Amendments

In rare and exceptional circumstances, as deemed appropriate by **The Bearded One**, an additional Beard Touch may be granted, subject to mutual agreement between **Facial Hair Enthusiast** and **The Bearded One**. Such an amendment must be executed in writing or with full verbal consent from all parties involved.

THE SLIDE BACK TO
CALIFORNIA

Is This Enough Space?

I watch the words fill the box reserved for my unsent text message and the cursor blinking back at me. A not exactly breakup text in progress, taunting me in the middle of a Starbucks. It couldn't possibly get more cliché than that. The only difference between me and everyone else who breaks up with someone over text is that Jonas and I aren't even officially dating yet. I quickly add to the thread of sent text messages.

Healthy things need room to breathe.

How poetic of me. As if I were a flower being smothered by a six-foot-one gardener who lives in Kansas, giving me nothing but everything I've ever wanted in a relationship.

That seems about right.

I am so accustomed to being treated like someone's secret that I can't fathom being loved out in the open for everyone to see. From my very first encounter with Jonas until now, he has been fiercely generous with his affection toward me. It all feels too good to be true. *He* feels too good to be true.

It makes sense to leave him now.

We've not even kissed. I don't know what it's like to hold his hand. My face doesn't know what it feels like to be brought in so close to him that I would rather not exist at all than exist apart from him.

If you don't count four-hour video calls in the middle of the night as quality time, then we're practically strangers. Strangers who need more than the existing fifteen hundred miles of space that already live between them...

I shut the notebook I'd been journaling in when I came to the conclusion that spending another moment talking to Jonas would only result in heartbreak. This is for the best, and I have no other choice than to believe that.

(Never mind that I'm too afraid to let myself sit still long enough to realize that I might feel like I've made a terrible decision.)

"Elyse?" I hear an almost familiar voice calling out from the long line forming at the cash register. "Elyse *Jones*? I thought that was you! I would recognize your curly hair anywhere!"

Either he's obsessed with me and has committed my appearance from every angle to memory, or he's kept up with me on social media. Somehow both are equally as flattering (and they shouldn't be).

The face I'm looking at belongs to a boy I had a crush on for roughly five minutes when we went to high school together. He is the brother of an acquaintance, and the last time I saw him he was much less attractive, with a mouthful of metal and rubber bands. These last ten years have been kind to him, and I'm having a hard time reconciling the boy I used to know in high school with the man standing in front of me.

"...Steven? Oh my...god, what a surprise. How are you?"

"I'm good! Very good. Even better now! How are you? Can I sit?"

His question is apparently rhetorical, because he is already pulling up a chair. Steven continues his rapid-fire questions.

"Do you live around here? You live in Australia, don't you? Do you love it? What is it like? How long are you in town? *How long have you been gone?*"

Whenever I'm presented with multiple questions in a row, I never know how to answer them. Do I string every single one of them in a row in the same order they were asked? Do I just answer the last one? What's the proper protocol here?

"I'm good! Sure. Not really. I just moved back. Yes. Sunny and gorgeous. Only a few months before I move to Texas. *Three years!*"

I opt for rapid-fire answers, matching his level of enthusiasm and speed. I watch him try to match which answers belong to which questions, then give up entirely. I hesitate to ask him any follow-up questions about himself, partly because I don't know enough about Steven anymore to think of something meaningful to ask him. But the bigger reason is that if I throw the conversation ball back into his court, it will keep him at this table longer than I'd like him to be.

I can almost see the awkward silence growing between us, right on top of this two-person table. If this were any other day, my need to be *liked* would overshadow my need to be *alone*. As a result, this solo trip would naturally convert itself into a very bizarre catch-up between two people who would otherwise have no reason to share a beverage of any kind. But as delighted as I would normally be to see my former-crush-now-stranger, I came here to be by myself and pretend I'm making progress at processing the raging dumpster fire of thoughts about a boy in Kansas that are currently taking up an uncomfortable amount of room in my mind.

I look at my phone, remembering the message I sent to Jonas right before I ran into Steven.

No response. That's...good, right? Is that good? Or is that very, very bad? An emotion (regret) that I'm unable (unwilling) to categorize has expanded in my chest, and I can feel it beginning to make its way into my stomach. Granted, it's been all of six minutes since I sent that message, which isn't nearly long enough to worry if Jonas is ignoring me or not. Then again, I asked for space. So if he *was* ignoring me, wouldn't I be getting exactly what I asked for?

I wish I'd never sent that text, and that's why I'm very glad I did.

"I've recently gotten into sword making."

Well. If there was anything Steven could have said to immediately pull me out of a thought spiral, that'll do it.

I slowly lift my face and trail my eyes over Steven's expression before asking for more information. His face is incredibly void of any telling emotions, which makes me wonder if I heard him correctly.

"I'm sorry...did you just say *sword* making?"

"Yes! Sword making! I've gotten really into woodworking and welding. I make swords in my free time. Do you want to see? They're really cool!"

His face lights up with pride as he talks about his hobby, and it's a nice sight. Steven's face is already attractive *without* the joy that's currently overtaking it, but this excitement is a good look on him too. I hear myself say, "Sure." I want to be alone, but my curiosity is forcing me to see this situation all the way to the end.

I'm not going to let someone tell me they're into sword making and then *not* ask to see a picture.

What a perfectly strange distraction from my current situation.

Without skipping a single beat, Steven pushes his chair away from the table and stands up. I was expecting him to reach for his phone and begin scrolling through photos of handmade swords. Instead he says, "Follow me! I have one in the trunk of my car!"

"No..."

...is what I *should* have said.

"OKAY!" is what actually leaves my mouth. People Pleaser Mode™ has officially been engaged. I'm almost positive that I'm either going to be kidnapped *or* shown a body part Steven has affectionately nicknamed his "Sword." The closer we get to the coffee shop exit, the louder I can hear my brothers yelling at me in my mind.

"I was actually on my way to deliver this custom piece to the person who just bought it. I only came in to grab my green tea and was going to leave, but then I saw you!" I have no idea which part of that sentence feels safest to address, if any part at all. What I do know is this: Steven preferring to drink hot green tea over literally any other beverage on a day when it's ninety-five degrees outside is somehow less shocking than it should be.

We push our way through the glass door with a considerable amount of effort, and my entire body is shoved backward by a warm wall of dry wind. I hate the heat, but I've always had a special place in my heart for the Santa Ana winds, which feel *so very*

California in this present moment. I've already been back for nine days, but this is the first time I've really felt happy to be here.

"I'm right here." He gestures to the silver Honda Accord parked right in front. If I had to guess, it was built sometime in the early 2000s. We're still so close to the coffee shop that I can see the whites of the eyes of customers sitting at the tables along the window. I decide right then and there to use this as my very level-headed reason for accepting such an outrageous offer, should anyone question my survival skills at a later date.

Sure enough, Steven opens the trunk of his car and reveals a very real, very non-metaphorical sword. The handle is made of dark red wood, smooth and shiny like it's been polished and sealed with a glaze. The metal blade is long, sharp, and it's...I mean, it's a sword.

A real Sword.

And Steven just pulled it from the trunk of his car.

"This is...not...*at all*...what I was expecting." Nothing about that declaration sounded like a compliment, but Steven thanks me anyway.

"The look on your face when I said I make swords told me as much." He releases a self-deprecating laugh into the warm air, which gives me permission to do the same. But my body is flooded with so much relief that I laugh twice as loud and twice as long as he does.

All at once the full realization of the last fifteen minutes falls on me.

I feel so homesick. How is that even possible? I'm in California, and California is home.

At least...it should feel like home, shouldn't it?

I feel so homesick I could cry.

Steven is telling me the story of how he got into the hobby of sword making. I'm doing my best to pay attention, but my best is to pretend. I don't want to be here anymore. At the coffee shop. In California. In this country, even. I miss my home, and apparently my heart has decided that "home" is Australia. I knew I loved living there, but I didn't know I'd feel lost like this, trying to belong anywhere else.

Elyse, stop it.

California was always supposed to be a quick pit stop before moving to Texas to finish my degree. I don't need California to feel like home. I need *Texas* to feel like home.

And I'm sure it will.

Because why wouldn't it?

I can make Texas feel like home...right?

I'm sure I can.

I hope I can.

I check my phone again for a response from Jonas, but the only thing worth noting is the time. Steven is somewhere in the middle of his Sword Making Origin Story, and I have no choice but to interrupt.

"I'm so sorry, but I didn't realize what time it was. I was supposed to be at someone's house a few minutes ago." I try to sound as happy as Steven expects me to be.

"Oh, no worries! I should get going too. This guy's owner"—he raises the sword slightly into the air with an affectionate sway—"is probably wondering where he is. He has a new home now."

I am willing to bet every single one of the ninety dollars in my bank account that Steven has given this sword a human nickname and is struggling to part ways with it. I don't blame him.

"Great to see you. I'll..." My initial instinct is to finish my sentence by saying, *I'll see you around.* But something about the interaction we just had tells me that would be as good as a handwritten invitation to see each other again *on purpose*. I would prefer to avoid being asked out on a date by Steven, mostly because I am wildly incapable of saying no. I think I was born without that gene.

"I'll go find my car now" is what I end up saying instead. Equally as natural of a goodbye if you don't think about it.

Eventually I *do* find my car. I climb inside, buckle my seat belt, and don't start the engine. I sit in a very warm Toyota RAV4 in complete silence. I stare at the steering wheel as if it's going to start talking any minute now.

Maybe it can tell me how to stop feeling so sad.

"I'm sorry I'm late! I ran into..." I look down at my hands and realize it looks like I made myself late to Tessa's house because I stopped for an iced coffee and then didn't even have the decency to ask if she wanted anything. "This coffee didn't make me late, a sword made me late. I was already *drinking* this coffee when the sword happened."

"A...s-sword?" Tessa is holding her new baby in her arms, and her shirt is covered in stains I would rather not know the origin of. I feel like an asshole for not thinking about bringing her a coffee.

"I don't want to talk about the sword. Here, take this." I hand over my drink; I've taken a total of two sips from it since ordering, because between all the Space and the Swords, I forgot my coffee existed.

Tessa is seven years older than me. We met at a restaurant we both used to work at and became friends instantly. Somewhere along the way, she adopted me as her little sister. With three brothers who are much older than I am, I'd always craved the kind of relationship I have with Tessa. I feel comfortable running to my brothers for advice about *anything*, knowing they'll have wisdom to share when I need it (and sometimes even when I don't). For most things, their insight is more than sufficient. But sometimes I really need advice that doesn't land in the ballpark of "Fuck 'em" or "It could be worse."

"I know you didn't get this coffee for me, but thank you anyway." She takes a sip that lasts so long that I wonder if she's trying to chug the entire thing all at once. There isn't much that Tessa would consider off-limits when trying to make me laugh, so a spur-of-the-moment chug wouldn't surprise me at all.

"Sit," she commands, pointing in the direction of her couch. I carefully step over the minefield of children's toys scattered on the floor and make my way across the living room. I can feel her eyes on me as I get situated. I'm afraid to look all the way up, to give her access to my entire face, which is undoubtedly displaying all the emotions I'm attempting to hide until I'm ready to talk.

"So how are y—"

"Please don't. You are so bad at small talk. Please...do not start with small talk. I love you and you don't need to pretend with me."

"Noted."

I've been gone for a long time. I'd forgotten what it was like to be insulted and then told I'm loved exactly the way that I am all in one breath. It's harsh and very refreshing, which sums up Tessa *perfectly*.

"To summarize: I like a boy. He likes me back, maybe even more than I like him. I got scared. I ran away. Figuratively, not literally. Maybe literally as well, I don't know. Either way, I think I regret it. Boom, you're all caught up."

Not a single reaction comes from the kitchen, from Tessa *or* Riley. It's as if her son had been briefed on my fear of long-term commitment before I got here, and this comes as no surprise to either of them. Many seconds pass before Tess opens her mouth to speak, then she closes it immediately.

More silent seconds.

So many more than I'd prefer.

"Okay," she finally says.

And then she says nothing else.

"Okay? What do you mean, *okay*?"

"It sounds like you've figured it out yourself. You regret it. What do you want me to say, that I agree with you?"

"I mean...I don't know? Do you think I *should* regret it? Usually you have a lot to say, but *today* is the day you decide you're suddenly the silent type? Usually you'd be telling me to stop being an idiot by now. To call him and tell him someone stole my phone and responded to hundreds of my unread texts for me. Tell him to disregard any messages he might or might not have received from a very polite thief in the last hour, *especially if they have anything to do with space!*"

"Elyse...you didn't even ask me a question. I don't have a clue who you're talking about."

I realize this is the first time I've talked to *anyone* about Jonas. I want to vomit at the thought of trying to catch her up on an entire month's worth of FaceTime calls, texts, and mini emotional breakdowns about a boy who lives in Kansas. I tell her everything as quickly and as honestly as I can. I've lied to myself about my feelings for Jonas *so many times* over the last few weeks that I'm finding it hard to tell the truth, even right now. Even when I really want to. All my thoughts are spilling out of me in no particular order. I sound like I'm having a heated argument with myself. Tessa does her best to piece together the information I'm giving her, using my quarter-baked context clues.

"Just take a deep breath."

I stop talking midsentence and follow her instructions.

Deeply, I breathe in.

Two.

Three.

Four.

A few seconds go by, and I'm holding the oxygen in my lungs, waiting for further instructions that never come. We're staring at each other in silence, expecting the other to say something.

"Jesus, Elyse. Breathe *out* too. I figured that was implied."

I breathe out as I'm instructed.

I'm tempted to recap everything I've shared: the grocery store, the shirtless beard-shaving at four in the morning over FaceTime, all of it. Even the Like I have for Jonas that's growing in my heart by the minute, and the space I just requested as a result.

But now that it's all out of me, I can't possibly say everything again, and as honestly as I did the first time. I don't trust myself not to smooth the emotion out of my story and soften the edges of my genuine feelings, which feel impossibly sharp and dangerous right now. If I'm good at anything, it's downplaying my feelings (negative and positive alike) in order to protect myself from the heartbreak I expect to be hiding around every corner.

Tessa can see how close all my competing emotions are to spilling out of my eyes. She walks through The Obstacle Course in her living room without ever looking down. I think her feet have memorized the path by now. She sits next to me on the couch—close enough to tell me she's there, but not so close that it feels like her presence is suffocating me. It's gestures like these that make me wonder if Tessa can read my mind.

"What *exactly* do you need right now? Because judging from your impression of me back there, it sounds like you know *exactly* how you feel. If you want someone to listen while you talk, I can do that. If you want advice, then ask me a question. But right now, you're just…angry."

She's right.

She's always right.

I quickly filter through all my thoughts and try prioritizing a list of questions from most to least urgent. "Do you think I'm wasting my time talking to someone who lives in another state?"

"I think that's a great question. Let's think about that for a second."

She takes a moment to form her answer in her head before she says it out loud—a skill I admire and don't altogether understand. I restrain myself from filling the dead space with words just because the space is there, and I'm nervous. I realize I haven't checked my phone for new messages since arriving at Tessa's house. I pull my phone out of my back pocket and try to make sense of the stack of notifications filling my home screen.

"Oh my god. OHMYGOD." Before I can read any of the messages, I launch my phone across the room. It lands somewhere behind a wicker basket of gigantic Legos.

"What?! What the fuck was that?!"

A combination of my sudden movement and the loud

THWHACK! of my phone hitting the ceramic floor tiles causes Riley to start crying. Until now he's been shockingly docile.

"I don't know, I panicked!"

"Clearly!" she shoots back as she stands up and starts shushing and swaying Riley back to sleep.

"I'm so sorry. My god, *I am so sorry.* Is he okay? I didn't mean to scare him. I just—"

"Panicked? Got it. Is your *phone* okay?" By the sound it made when it hit the ground, I highly doubt it. I run across the room, stumbling through The Obstacle Course, and barely make it to where my phone landed without rolling my ankle. I examine my phone from front to back, looking for anything that resembles a very expensive spiderweb on either side as I rescue it from the floor.

"The phone is fine," I say, relieved. If I wasn't so embarrassed that my first instinct when I get texts I'm too nervous to open is to *chuck my phone across the room*, I'd be impressed with the softball skills resurrecting themselves from the hobby graveyard lingering in my body.

"I'm guessing Jonas texted you back?"

"Yes."

Tessa is swaying, and Riley is almost all the way settled. She's looking at me like I'm a Season Finale cliffhanger on one of her favorite shows. I don't think she's been around this much real-life drama since the going-away party she threw me before I moved to Australia. We took shots of spiked lavender lemonade and drunk-texted my exes to see who would respond first. The canyon between her life three years ago and her life right now is suddenly very obvious to me. The only thing different about me is that I have a couple more exes to add to the list, and now I can legally take shots.

"*Hello?* Are you going to *read* Jonas's messages? Preferably *out loud*?"

I tap on the most recent notification, and our conversation thread fills my screen. It reveals a long string of new texts, all sent one after another. I read them one at a time, first to myself and then out loud for Tessa to hear.

Healthy things need room to breathe.

Today, 11:20AM

Jonas

Hey I'm sorry I didn't respond sooner!

I'm over at my friend Mike's house, we're catching up!

I know you JUST asked for space, and I completely understand. So let me go ahead and acknowledge that what I'm about to ask you seems ... insane.

I'm actually still here at Mike's house. I was telling him about you and then out of the blue, he asked if he could fly you to Kansas so you and I can hang out in person.

I guess he has all these airline miles because he flies so much for work? He has his computer out right now and he's literally looking up flights.

Jonas

How would you feel about spending a week with me in Kansas? We can get to know each other in person. if you decide you like me, great! if it turns out you don't, that's fine too. But at least you'd know for sure.

He just said he's looking at flights in August. Maybe some time around your birthday? (I swear this was his idea.)

What do you think?

If the idea of this is too much or you need some time to think about it, that's totally okay! I'm sure this feels like a lot.

Just promise me you'll think about it?

Today, 12:14 PM

Please don't be mad, but... Mike bought a couple of flight options just in case! You totally don't have to use them if you don't want to use them. There is NO pressure here. But the flights are yours if you want them. :)

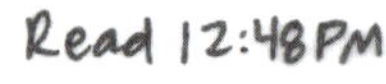

We don't say anything for a handful of minutes. Maybe a couple handfuls of minutes, it's hard to tell. In complete silence, we stare at each other. We are both unsure of *how* or *where* to start. The longer I take to speak, the less I'm sure of what to say.

Tessa breaks through first, her voice a *barely there* whisper. "So..."

"So that's...th-that is...I mean, that is...*really*, like..." I start to second-guess my understanding of what I just read and maybe my ability to read at all. I decide to go through the messages quietly to myself for a third time.

Just to make sure.

You can never be too sure.

AND I AM NOT EVEN A LITTLE BIT SURE OF ANYTHING AT THE MOMENT.

My legs are having a bit of trouble keeping me upright, so I plop myself on the ground, Criss Cross Applesauce. The tiles are cold underneath me, and I wonder what it would feel like to press my face against them. I think that would feel nice.

I think I'm overwhelmed, and I think that would feel very nice.

I think the tiles are dirty, and I think I don't care.

I lie on my stomach and half of my face is touching the tiles now.

I was right, this feels very nice.

Tessa has remained quiet, completely unfazed that I'm lying on her kitchen floor. She's still swaying from side to side with Riley in her arms, waiting for me to mentally come back into the same room as her.

I open my mouth to speak. This time a fully formed question comes out. "Did Jonas just...did he just invite me to spend a week with him in Kansas?"

"No, babe. He didn't. *He bought you a plane ticket* to Kansas."

I want to laugh, because if this were happening to anyone else, *everything* about this would be very funny. *What a perfect Hallmark movie this would make,* I think. *And also a very predictable plot of a True Crime Podcast,* I think immediately after that, probably even a little bit louder than the thought before it.

"Fuck the space. Forget about it. You're going to Kansas, right? Please tell me you're going to Kansas. I mean, who turns down a free trip to Kansas?"

"A *free trip to Kansas*?" Now I am genuinely laughing. This has officially become All the Way Funny. "I mean this with all the respect in the world, but...what the hell am I going to do in Kansas? I have spent a grand total of fifteen minutes in the same room as Jonas. I like him, yes—"

"YoulikehimSOmuch!" she quickly adds in between my thoughts.

"All right, yes, I like him *SO much*. Fine. But I can't just *go to Kansa—*"

"FUCK THE SPACE, ELYSE. YOU'RE GOING TO KANSAS."

THE STAIRCASE TO KANSAS

My Very Last First Kiss

Jonas is sitting dangerously close to me on his basement couch. I can smell the honey whiskey on his breath and the pomade he swiped through his hair this morning. He's never seemed taller than he does right now, even sitting down. When I turn my head to look at him—which I've been avoiding at all costs—I have to tilt my head upward just to make eye contact with him. The safest place for me to look right now is straight ahead.

So that's exactly where I look.

I can confidently say I've never examined an unlit fireplace with as much focus and intensity as I am studying the fireplace directly in front of me.

I've only been here for twelve hours, but I already can't remember why I warned Jonas that he wasn't allowed to kiss me as I was boarding my plane at LAX. *"Don't hold my hand. Don't kiss me. I'm not your girlfriend. I'm just trying to figure things out, and kissing will just confuse me."* It's safe to say that I've figured a few things out since arriving. One of them being: I wish I wasn't an idiot, and I *really wish* I didn't tell him not to kiss me. Unfortunately, I'm stubborn enough to follow through with this ridiculous rule, which I made for *absolutely* no legitimate reason.

(Other than the fact that I am terrified of healthy relationships and will do almost anything to get in my own way and then wonder where it all went wrong.)

We've been talking for hours down here in the basement. I feel the drink we shared earlier warming my body in a way that isn't unpleasant at all. Hours of The Question Game have allowed my mind to detangle itself and instruct my body to relax. I want to tell him that I like Kansas and that I like him even more. I want to tell him that I could see myself living somewhere like this one day, especially if he was there too. I want to tell him so many things, but with him sitting so close to me, I find it incredibly hard to say anything other than "Very cool basement. Wish we had these in California."

"You don't have basements in California?"

"Not that I know of. Aren't these for, like, tornadoes and stuff?"

"They are, yeah. I guess I didn't think about it, but California doesn't have tornadoes. I guess you wouldn't need basements."

Perfect, we're talking about the weather.

Tornados are, objectively, very Unsexy. In any other case, Unsexy conversations with a person you are so attracted to you can barely breathe wouldn't be considered a positive thing. If I were to make a Pros and Cons list titled ***"First Date?"*** you definitely wouldn't catch me celebrating while writing in the pros column:

We talked about tornadoes! It turned both of us off—right away!

But nothing about what's happening right now is typical. I'll take all the help I can get while trying to follow the absurd rules Elyse From Twelve Hours Ago decided were important enough to create. Besides...is this even a first date? Like, would this be considered The World's *Longest* First Date? Did the date start the minute my plane landed in Kansas? Or does Jonas have to specifically *ask* me on a date for it to be considered a date? Maybe there needs to be a restaurant and some version of a fancy outfit involved for it to actually count.

I suddenly feel very unsure of how to categorize this time with Jonas. I assume these are things any sane person thinks through *before* getting on a plane to spend a week with a boy they are *In Like* with. As a rule, I'm generally concerned about everything.

All the time.

But right now, I'm realizing that I lack the focus and emotional maturity required to channel my unnecessary and constant concern into something *helpful.*

Like—oh, I don't know—thinking through a game plan for after I arrived in Kansas.

Today has felt like three days. If I know anything about game plans (and I promise I don't), then a full night's sleep will help me get myself in order for tomorrow.

More important: the faster I get into my room, the likelihood of my mouth slamming into Jonas's mouth decreases considerably. At least...for tonight.

I stand up and step away from the couch we've sunken into over the last two hours. I'm almost positive we were farther away from each other when we sat down, but every time one of us asked a new question, the space between us became less and less. It happened so slowly that I didn't notice, until I wasn't able to notice anything else.

I stretch my arms up high and yawn, which makes Jonas yawn. Which makes us laugh for no reason other than we like sharing something.

Even if it's only a yawn.

I begin walking toward the bedroom his family has been kind enough to let me use for the week. When I first was shown to my room earlier today, the idea of sleeping down in the basement was terrifying (a definite point in the True Crime Podcast column), but now I'm grateful for the physical space separating me from the rest of the people in this house. Two floors separating me and a sleeping Jonas is about as much space as I'd like moving forward.

"I like Kansas," I finally say, still walking toward my bedroom. I can feel Jonas walking closely behind me, like he's dropping me off at my front door after taking me out to dinner. Except dinner had been cooked by his mom and eaten at his childhood dining room table.

With his entire immediate family.

So this *is* considered a date!

"I'm glad you like Kansas. I like having you in Kansas. Looks good on you."

A single gust of wind could snap my self-control in half. I need to get myself on the other side of this bedroom door, or else Elyse From Twelve Hours Ago is going to be very disappointed in me. Out of all the versions that exist of me at this current moment, Elyse From Twelve Hours Ago seems like the one who is thinking the clearest. As for the rest of us...it's not looking too good, because we're deeply infatuated and just a little bit buzzed.

I finally gather just enough courage to turn around and begin the process of saying good night to Jonas. I've mentally prepared myself for how close he'll be when I face him, but that doesn't keep my heart rate from spiking.

"Well, this is me." I jokingly point to the door of the bedroom I'm borrowing. I'm usually *very good* at ruining special moments like these with jokes that are *barely* funny. Most of the time it's by accident. This time it's on purpose.

This time, it doesn't work.

Jonas closes the space between us to less than an inch. I can feel the warmth of his body from here. I'm staring directly into the center of his chest, afraid to look up at him. Knowing What Happens Next if I do. Wanting What Happens Next to happen more than anything I've ever wanted What Happens Next in my entire life. Somewhere between fifteen and two thousand seconds pass without either of us saying a word, standing as still as we possibly can. And then even more still than that.

I'm resting all my weight against the crown molding of the doorway behind me, while Jonas leans his hand against the wall beside me. He tilts his face down to mine ever so slightly. I can feel his breath on my lips.

His face is so close to mine that my eyes instinctively close all on their own.

"Can I kiss you?" Jonas asks in a whisper that is *so ridiculously far* from being Unsexy, it almost hurts.

I take the deepest of breaths, inhaling as much of his scent as I can, then open my eyes and summon a level of superhuman strength that I imagine the human body reserves for people who lift cars off other people, or campers who fight bears and make it out alive.

"You promised me you wouldn't," I manage to finally say back. My words hold the least amount of conviction that words can possibly hold before they don't even count as words anymore. Jonas hasn't moved his face away from mine, but I watch his jaw flex, *just barely*, the moment my words register. He closes his eyes and puts just enough space between our lips to make sure I knew he heard me.

That I knew he was *listening*.

That I knew I was safe to say no.

That I wouldn't be asked again, because saying "no" one time is *enough*.

"You're right. I *did* promise you that." He shoves his hands in his pockets and steps farther away from me—this time putting half a basement's worth of space between us, allowing both of us to remember how to breathe and think properly again.

He continues to face me as he slowly walks backward toward the basement staircase. Tonight and every other kiss-less night, until I say otherwise. His eyes are dancing between my face and the carpet underneath our feet. I can't tell whether I'm seeing embarrassment, recalibration, or a little bit of both flashing across his face.

"I'm sorry," I allow myself to say out loud, *just once*. Because I *am* sorry I made that stupid rule for myself. And I'm especially sorry that I made it from a place of fear. But something I'm *not* sorry for is following through with it. If this is forever, then there's no need to rush.

"You have nothing to be sorry for. Good night, Elyse. I can't wait to see you in the morning." Jonas stands on the bottom step of the staircase and smiles in a way that reassures me nothing between us has changed. He waits for me to walk into my bedroom and close the door before making his way upstairs for the rest of the night.

The sound of his footsteps fades away to nothing, and I'm still staring at the back of the door. I can't move, and I don't want to. Maybe if I continue standing here, just inches away from where we just were, I can pretend I didn't say no. If I close my eyes and replay tonight in my mind, maybe I can pretend he kissed me, or that I wasn't so afraid of letting him that I built a wall of rules around me to ensure that he wouldn't get close enough to my heart to break it.

"Can I kiss you?"

"You promised me you wouldn't."

I'm not entirely sure, but I think I'm going to cry now.

I launch myself onto the bed with as much force as I possibly can. The white metal bed frame is still squeaking back and forth from the impact of my crash landing. I smash my face into a pile of quilted throw pillows until I can barely breath. The further I can bury my head into these decorative pillows, the less real any of this feels. The hand-embroidered pillowcases smell like mothballs, and for some reason, I like that very much.

"Can I kiss you?"

"You promised me you wouldn't."

A sea of mismatched colors, patterns, and textures are swallowing me. I'm exhausted, a little bit sunburned, and a lotta bit sure that I am going to kiss Jonas before the week is over.

"Can I kiss you?"

"You promised me you wouldn't."

"You're right. I did *promise you that."*

____ sleep.

I kissed Jonas on the basement couch the next day.

Cows, On Purpose.

August 24, 2016

I've been here for two days. If you would have asked me to point to Kansas on a map a month ago, I would have looked at you and apologized for being geographically inept. I also would have asked you why you needed to know where Kansas is, or why anyone would need to know where Kansas is . . . except perhaps Wizard of Oz enthusiasts?

Yet here I am. In the guest bedroom of the Myers family home. In Kansas. Somewhere in the middle of the country. That feels specific enough, doesn't it?

There are cows, like, fifty feet away from me. Cows that are there on purpose. BECAUSE JONAS AND HIS FAMILY OWN THEM.
I watched one of them get impregnated yesterday. (By a man with a really long glove.) I didn't know if walking away in the middle of it would distract the cow and the man with the long glove, so instead, I just stood still. Maybe more still

than I've ever stood in my entire life? The last thing I'm going to do is be the person responsible for spooking a cow that's being artificially inseminated. Listen... whether I walked away at that point or not, the memory was already branding itself into the folds of my brain. I decided I had to see it all the way through. I washed that experience down with my first ever glass of honey whiskey. If Jonas was ~~traumitized~~ impacted by that experience even half as much as I was... he didn't show it at all.

I'm having a very hard time believing this is actually happening. All of this. Everything. It's all so QUICK!

I can't tell if it's too quick or if it's the exact right speed and I'm just scared. The cow thing definitely happened too quickly. But the rest of it? I'm not entirely sure. Part of me wanted to prolong this weird in-between that we've been living in for the past few months. Where there are four states and fifteen hundred miles of space between us. The part where I still get to be everything he thinks I am, and maybe even more. The part where if we break up, there's nothing at all to break.

I was so scared I would spend five days here and he would eventually realize I'm not as he imagined I'd be. What if I let him down? I have a million different versions of myself that I wear for the benefit of others. But with Jonas, none of them seem to fit. Five days is a very long time to pretend, and the weird thing is... I don't know if I even want to pretend.

When I'm with Jonas, all of those alternate versions of myself feel like a mask I'm suffocating under. I care less about look and more about the way I feel when I'm around him. That's exactly why I'm scared. Because every other person who's walked away from me has been walking away from a version of me that barely exists.

But I'm not pretending with Jonas.
I'm not even sure I can.
That means if he leaves, he's leaving me.
If he stays, he's choosing me.
Why do both of those outcomes scare me so much?!

When Jonas first asked me to come to Kansas, I said I needed time to think about it. He understood. Who wouldn't need time to think about a decision like that?? I mean .. other than him. He just seems so sure about me, all the time. How can he be so sure?

As I drove home from Tessa's, I realized that if I was actually considering spending the week with Jonas, it would probably be a good time to fill my mom in on who Jonas is. Or, you know, that he even exists. I definitely hadn't imagined our first conversation about him ending with "... and I think I'm flying to Kansas for a week to see him?"

I'm not sure what it says about me that my mom was less surprised by what's happening here than I was. Am I really the only one who thinks this is at least a little bit crazy? Between Tessa's and my mom's reactions, I seem to be the outlier here. I mean... objectively speaking, this is a little crazy. Am I missing something? Can it really be that simple? Even Jonas's parents don't seem to be fazed by my being here. A near stranger, sleeping in a spare bedroom in their basement. Spending five days in their house to test-drive their son for a potential future together.

I need at least one person to confirm that this is sort of (if not completely) NUTS.

I thought about Jonas the rest of the day after he asked me to fly here to Kansas. I tried to go on a run to clear my head, but I only made it about a half a mile before sitting down on a park bench and reading through his messages one more time. The twentieth time through didn't uncover any information I hadn't already learned from the first nineteen times I read them. But reading the words that Jonas wrote made my chest feel a little less tight.

I walked back home, took a shower, then spent the rest of the night reading his messages. Late that night, I called Jonas to tell him my decision.

Me: I guess I'll see you in Kansas.

Jonas: Are you serious? You're really coming?

Me: Of course. Who would turn down a free trip to Kansas?!

I tried my hardest to infuse the same level of enthusiasm that my mom and Tessa both seemed to have about free vacations to the middle of nowhere. After we stopped laughing, Jonas said The Very Best and Most Perfectly Right Thing anyone could have ever said to me in that moment.

"We aren't in High School anymore, Elyse. I like you. I want to be with you. I'm not going to pretend I don't. I want you to be as sure about me as I am about you. That can't happen if we aren't in the same place for at least a few days in a row. So even if you get here and you realize you don't like me as much as you originally imagined, at least I got to have five beautiful days with you."

When he was done speaking, every atom of pressure that I'd felt slowly crushing me from the inside out suddenly evaporated. When we hung up the phone, I wrote down every word I could remember from our conversation so I'd be able to keep it forever. Between that and his texts, I decided I might just print everything he sends me and place it all in a binder, a makeshift book I can read to myself about a boy from Kansas who likes me more than he probably should.

Even if we don't end up together, I always want to remember what this feels like – to be wanted by Jonas Myers <u>this</u> <u>much</u>.

Elyse Myers has a pretty good ring to it!
Oh my god, stop. I did not just write that.

THE PAPER AIRPLANE BACK TO

CALIFORNIA

To whom it will never concern,

A story lived here once.

I want you—specifically you, the person my life has never and will never concern—to know that the story I willingly redacted from this creative canon of my memories is so perfectly heart-breaking that I have lost sleep writing it and reading it and reading it back again.

It is beautiful because what came after you made the memory of this story beautiful.

It is beautiful in spite of you, and it always will be.

It is beautiful because it exists and you will never get to read it.

I will tell this omitted story in the future, one hundred different ways. Each one of them laid out so perfectly and so strategically and so fictionally that you will feel all the heartbreak and none of the glory. You will be stripped from it completely, and only the memory of your hurt will remain in me. I will create characters and scenes and stories and art that have the DNA of your terrible decisions embedded into them while the person of you will be forgotten.

Elyse before you; Elyse after you.

With this letter, those people will reintroduce themselves and become one.

When you buy this book and flip through the pages to find a reference to your existence in my life, you will find this letter instead.

I hope it disappoints you.

I hope you are happy and healthy and thriving and just mildly disappointed. Just today. Not every day, but just—and especially—today, for the few moments that come after reading this page in my book.

You will never find yourself in anything that I make, because this is not about you. I do not know you. I have never met you. I forget you exist. You are forgotten.

With Nothing,
Elyse

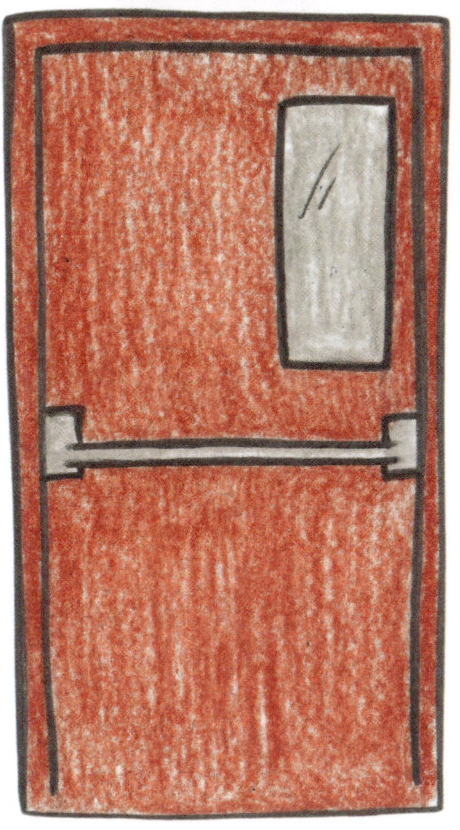

THE EMERGENCY EXIT TO

TEXAS

Maybe I Will

My eyes are tired and I'm struggling to see everything as clearly as I should. As I get out of my car, I can see the shape of Jonas walking toward me. I rub my eyes to get a better look at him. I've been dreaming about seeing him in person for weeks, and I don't want to miss a single second of him now that he's actually in front of me.

I've been driving since sunrise and now it's nearly set, but even exhaustion can't slow the excitement that's flooding my body as I remember what it's like to be near Jonas and feel his warmth as he pulls me into one of his hugs.

I shut my car door and start walking toward him, jumping up and down to show how happy I am to see him. Well, see a *shadow of him* that soon won't be a shadow anymore. There's nearly a football field's worth of distance between the lot where I parked and the front door he's just left. I have no idea who all these cars belong to. Why are there so many cars between us, and where did all these people come from?

When he gets a little closer, I begin waving to get his attention. The visual static that I can't rub out of my eyes is making it look as though he's staring right past me as I wave.

Maybe I should have taken a few more breaks while driving up here. I can hardly see anything at this point. Only a few cars' worth of distance are between us now, and I can't wait for a hug any longer. I begin running toward him, stopping right before my body collides into his.

"HELLO, KIND STRANGER!" I say, way louder than I mean to. My greeting echoes through the parking lot, and I hear the excitement in my voice four or five times before it rings out into nothing.

Jonas still hasn't made eye contact with me. He doesn't...notice me at all, actually. He looks straight through me as he sidesteps a few feet, then continues walking forward as if I'm just a weird stain on the concrete.

I force myself to laugh at the joke he's obviously making. It feels a *little* too cruel to be a joke, given the circumstances. I chase after him.

"Jonas! Hey!" I call out through another forced laugh. "You're taking the Stranger thing a little too seriously!" I finally catch up to him and put my hand on his forearm.

He turns around, and this time he's looking right at me. His eye contact is fierce, and he doesn't look happy to see me.

"Are you okay? Did something happen? You don't...look like yourself. You look really pale, actually."

I rub my eyes and try squinting to see if that might alleviate the static that's blocking my view of the most beautiful man in the world. It helps, but barely.

"Sorry, do I *know* you?"

What...the...hell? Why is he being so weird? I just drove from another state to see him, and he's acting like he has no clue who I am.

"Jonas, I know you're trying to be funny, but I'm actually really tired and a little bit sensitive right now. I just sat for, like, twelve hours in a car with a fabric top half that somehow doesn't latch all the way to the bottom half. So I've basically been listening to a high-pitched whistle since I left Texas this morning. At five. Before the sun was up. Can you at least give me a hug?"

"How do you know my name?"

My god. This dude really knows how to commit to a bit, doesn't he?

"You're breaking my heart a little bit. Can you please drop the joke for just a second? I drove all this way to see you."

If I didn't know any better, I'd say the face that's staring back at me right now *really* has no idea who I am.

"Holy shit, did you hit your head? Jonas. I'm, like, actually really worried. This isn't funny—"

"Stop using my name like you know who I am! I've never met you before!" He pulls his arm free and continues walking away.

I run to catch up to him one more time. I stop directly in front of him.

"Jonas! Do you really not remember me? Elyse? Your *girlfriend*? The other person in the photo on your home screen? You know, the girl in the picture who's pressing her mouth onto yours?"

I hold my phone up and start scrolling through photos of the last time we were together, which was also the *first* time we were together. I swipe through picture after picture of us. Wasting time in a coffee shop. Buying sodas on Mass Street. Eating tacos on a park bench. Sitting on his front porch drinking whiskey and watching the sunset.

Nothing.

His face looks just as empty, and his stare looks just as hollow.

I am so confused.

"You said you loved me." I am dangerously close to begging him to love me back, begging him to love me the way he loved me this morning when I called to tell him I was on my way to Omaha.

I begin to cry. I'm so tired that the tears sting as they make their way past my eyelids and fall down my face. It feels like someone took an eye dropper and placed water from the ocean directly into my eyeballs. I'm in so much pain—everywhere—that I can't decide what hurts the most.

The pain in my eyes, or the ache in my chest that's serving as a silent *I Told You So*. I knew it was only a matter of time before something like this happened. He was too good to be true.

Everything was too good to be true.

"I don't even know you. I can't love someone I don't know."

DEE-NEE-NEE-NEEEET

DEE-NEE-NEE-NEEEET

*DEE-NEE-NEE-NE—*THWACK**

Through barely open eyes, I look at my alarm clock. It reads 4:32 a.m. I'm usually a morning person, but the recent uptick of these recurring nightmares makes me feel a lot less excited to jump out of bed before the sun rises and convince myself that *it's going to be a great day!* Nothing feels great when your brain consistently waits until you're deep asleep to remind you of everything you've ever been insecure about, and then maybe even things you've never *thought* to be insecure about, but now you have a few extra things just in case!

You know...if the normal insecurities aren't doing the trick anymore.

I change out of my pajamas and double-check the bag I packed before going to sleep last night. I have a tendency to pack clothes I've never worn just in case I have a personality transplant when I get to wherever I'm going. I usually end up saying, "You just never know!" to myself as I'm rolling up a red sundress and throwing in high heels that I don't even like. I pull everything out of my suitcase that I have a zero percent chance of actually wearing.

After I turn on the coffeepot, I throw my backpack into the back seat of my car and load the front seat with snacks. I go back inside and lay my face on the kitchen counter as the carafe slowly fills with coffee. I've always enjoyed road trips, but I've never been quite as excited to get to my final destination as I am this morning.

This is going to be a *long* twelve hours.

I wonder what the Sun says to t

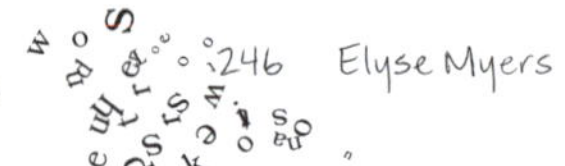

I wonder what the Sun says to the Moon when it takes its place in the sky—or if the Moon ever wishes it could trade places with the Sun to be awake during the day. Even just once. I wonder if the Moon has ever said to the Stars: "I liked this at the beginning, but I don't think I like it as much anymore." The Stars always shine brighter for the Moon, which is something the Moon has decided to love very much. But when the Stars say to the Moon, "The Day is only the Day when the Sun is out," does the Moon wish it made Its own light, just like the Sun? Does the Moon think: "Even a quarter of the Sun's light would be more than enough light for Me." I wonder what the Trees would say to the Birds if they could talk, because the Birds talk at the Seemingly Silent Trees all day. Do they understand that the Trees aren't able to talk back? Do the Birds feel ignored or do they chirp at the Trees: "Do you think you're better than us?" The Unsilent Trees reply: "Shwhshwshwshwshw."

I wonder if the Road ever gets too warm and asks the Sky to relay messages to the Sun? Messages like "Can you find somewhere else to shine today? I'm burning under Your watch!" Would the Sun move behind the Clouds and ask the Rain to give more of Itself than it had planned to give, simply for the sake of the Road? I wonder if the Sky enjoys being home to Everything. Does Everything get tired of being so vast that It almost doesn't exist at all? It never stops existing. How tired and lonely must the Sky be? I wonder if the Sky feels proud to be the keeper of All Things: the Moon that wishes It were the Sun; the Sun that gives light to the Moon that the Moon can't see; the Stars that glow just the same for the Sun; the Seemingly Silent Trees that are not silent at all but talk to the Birds in a language they don't understand; the Birds that have made themselves at home in the Trees; the Road that lives under the Sky who keeps All Things. I wonder if: my car is hurting the Road?

When my phone's map tells me I'm only twenty minutes from Jonas's apartment, I find one last gas station to stop at. I pull out my backpack and find the outfit I planned on wearing the very first time Jonas saw me after officially becoming his *girlfriend.*

Objectively, the outfit I chose to change into looks almost identical to the one I wore for the first eleven hours and forty minutes of the drive. The only major difference is the knit hoodie I pull over my head to complete my look. It's a deep maroon, and its previous owner is the very person I'm driving to see. Jonas let me borrow it so I'd have something of his while we were apart, and the thought of him seeing me in it makes my stomach do a million different things.

Part of me wants to wear his hoodie because it makes me feel safe. Most of me picked Jonas's sweater because my anxiety has convinced me that the nightmare I can't stop having is actually a premonition.

The *logical* part of my brain understands that these nightmares are about as cliché as it gets when it comes to anxious thoughts. But these dreams are happening for a reason, and whether they're a premonition (they aren't) or my brain's attempt at working out very real insecurities (this is the obvious answer), it doesn't make them feel any less real.

My daytime brain spends all day looking for proof that Jonas will leave.

My nighttime brain provides exactly *that*, every single night.

I get into my car and resume my drive. I know that the moment I see Jonas every insecurity my nightmare represents will dissolve into nothingness. They'll melt alongside everything else in my body when I see Jonas walking toward me. His real-life, fully human, non-digital body! And he isn't even inside a phone screen!

I'd assumed a twelve-hour road trip would be plenty of time to prepare myself to stand in front of my brand-new boyfriend. But as the map's ETA and the current time on my car's dash start getting closer and closer to each other, I feel myself panicking for no real reason.

You're not anxious, you're excited! Your brain just can't tell the difference!

I repeat this to myself as loud as I can without triggering the same genre of secondhand embarrassment I feel whenever I've slipped getting out of the shower and fallen onto the floor...naked. No one is there to witness it, but the part of me that feels like I'm in *The Truman Show* likes to remind me that nothing is impossible!

The sun is setting, and I hadn't considered how dark the middle of nowhere gets once the sun goes down. I'm only a mile and a half away from his apartment when the service on my phone starts to become unreliable. My map isn't exactly sure where we are, and I am very unfamiliar with the surface my tires are driving over right now. I stop driving, turn my high beams on, and try to see what, exactly, is lining the road underneath my tires.

Should I have gotten out of the car? No. Did I? I don't really feel like saying.

But yes, I did.

And as it turns out, I've never driven on gravel before. I had no idea cars could even *drive* over gravel, because I have never lived in a place where the streets are anything but streets. The kind of streets that every single street *should* be. Asphalt and...other street things that don't feel like anything at all when you drive over them! Definitely not like tiny little rocks that might not—but probably will—puncture holes in every single one of your tires before you even get the chance to see and hug and kiss your boyfriend in person for the *first time!*

And when I say *"first time!"* I obviously mean the first time as your *boyfriend*, not the first time *ever*, because you already saw and hugged and kissed A Boy From Kansas, and you liked it so much that he's now your boyfriend!

I get back into the car I may or may not have gotten out of and do the one thing that will not help me *at all* in this situation. ~~I start to cry. It's fine, I was fine, except I didn't feel fine for a second.~~ I pull myself together and back off the gravel as slowly as any car has ever driven in the history of cars, then pull back onto the main street, which is very gravel-less and a fraction more lit than the street—I'm being very generous with that term—I was just driving on.

I'm aware that I'm driving in the opposite direction that I should be driving, but I'm trying to find an area that my cell phone likes just enough to reconnect to a cell tower and save me from driving aimlessly in this vacuum of light that apparently happens when you get far enough away from major cities. My phone finds just enough service to reload my map, and while I'm at it, I try to find an alternate route that doesn't include driving on surfaces that will pop all four of my tires. I take screenshots of the map and the directions and study both for a few moments so I can get a better sense of where I'm going.

You're not anxious, you're excited! Your brain just can't tell the difference!

High beams on, I pull back onto the road and follow the alternate route to Jonas's apartment.

There are *exactly* zero cars in sight.

I'm now stopped in front of the road I'm meant to turn right onto.

And there's gravel on this one too.

You have got *to be kidding me.*

I am so overwhelmed by this devastating news that I don't even consider the possibility that cars are equipped to drive over surfaces much more atypical than gravel.

My body starts panicking very hard and very fast and very aggressively, and I can feel my brain trying to tell my body this situation is not worth *this* level of panic.

Well, my brain should probably speak up, because all I'm feeling is a bunch of judgment from the neck up and a shitstorm of panic from the neck down.

But I keep driving forward because Jonas is forward.

When I finally turn onto the road, my tires slip, and I struggle to gain the traction I need to feel comfortable continuing forward. When I pull my phone out to call Jonas and tell him what's happening, I have no service.

It's only a matter of time before I die out here, alone and in total darkness—oh, never mind, I see a car driving toward me on the other side of the road. The driver looks like they're handling it just fine and not at all on the verge of tears.

I guess the tiny gravel isn't a threat to my tires after all.

This is very good news!

I drive no faster than five miles per hour the entire three-quarters of a mile that this road lasts until it leads me into a very paved parking lot with only a few cars parked in it.

One of them being Jonas's navy blue HHR.

You're not anxious, you're excited!

Your brain just can't tell the difference!

I pull into a parking spot, and before I've even shut my engine off I can see Jonas walking through the glass doors of his building. I haven't seen him in person since I visited him on his family's farm in Kansas, which was two months ago. When he'd dropped me off at the airport, we were friends who'd kissed each other a few times and had a rough idea of what the future *could* look like.

Maybe.

Possibly.

If I am able to suspend my disbelief just long enough to avoid torpedoing this whole thing because I'm terrified of being abandoned—but that's fine.

But seeing Jonas walk toward me now, I realize how much has changed since then.

We've opened up to each other in ways I didn't think I was capable of opening up to someone. We've talked every night, all night. Way too late into the night, and sometimes until it was no longer night at all. We've shared the best and the worst of ourselves, and every mundane thing in between. The Jonas who's walking straight toward me across the World's Longest Lawn is a completely different person from the Boy From Kansas I'd spent five days with because he asked me to.

I yell over to him as I climb out of my car. "Were you just watching for my car through the window?" I laugh because I don't know how to process the flood of positive emotions that come with the mental image of Jonas sitting at his bedroom window, waiting for me to get here.

"If I said yes, would you think I'm pathetic?"

There's still so much lawn to be crossed before he's standing in front of me. Two thoughts run through my mind:

1. I'm not sure *why* I decided to park so far away from the front door when this parking lot is virtually empty.
2. This would now be a good time to start walking toward Jonas instead of standing next to my car, frozen in place like an idiot.

I try to move, but my body is too full of adrenaline. I can't do much of anything right now. Move. Breathe. Think. It all feels off the table right now. Apparently when my body is presented with the options to either Fight, Flight, or Freeze, its preference is to Freeze.

I am frozen. An ice sculpture that looks a lot like Elyse.

You're not anxious, you're excited! Your brain just can't tell the difference!

Jonas has now made it past The World's Longest Lawn and steps off the curb into the parking lot. When he walks under a streetlamp, he transforms from an outline of a person into the most beautiful human being my eyes have ever seen. I swear I can hear my heart beating in my ears as he gets closer.

"Could you have parked any farther away?" He's so close that I can hear the laugh that came with his question.

You're not anxious, you're excited!

Your brain just can't tell the difference!

Oh my god, I think I'm gonna—

FLIGHT.

I AM ALL FLIGHT.

I AM NO LONGER FREEZE.

I am Flighting so *fast*—and so unexpectedly—in the opposite direction of Jonas that I don't have time to consider where I'm going or why I'm Flighting in the first place. I just drove twelve hours to see my favorite person in the whole world. But as soon as he became a real person standing in front of me, my first instinct is to run away?

What the hell is wrong with me?

"I'M SORRY!" I shout without looking back at Jonas. I'm still running away. I feel my brain wanting so badly to disassociate from the events taking place, and I'm doing everything in my power to keep myself here mentally. Mentally *and* physically here, because something tells me that if I give my legs permission, they would run the rest of me all the way back to Irving, Texas.

I finally reach the end of the pavement and stop running. I look out into near Nothingness and feel my foot stepping onto the grass where the parking lot ends and the field and Nothingness begins.

"There's mice in that grass. I wouldn't do that if I were you."

I turn around and see Jonas a few paces behind me. My god, he really is the most beautiful man I've ever met. The adrenaline is wearing off, and I can finally make sense of all the small details of his face and hair and, well, everything else that makes Jonas *Jonas*.

"I'm not running away from you. I'm actually really excited to see you." My brain is giving me an instant replay of what I just did from about ten different camera angles. I'm watching it again in slow motion when Jonas bends down, hooks his right arm around the backs of my thighs, and effortlessly pulls my entire body onto his right shoulder. He begins carrying me back to my car.

"What are you *doing!*" I try to make my voice sound angry, but my enjoyment betrays me by cutting my sentence in half with a giggle that sounds like it belongs to someone a quarter my age.

"I'm making sure you don't run into the middle of a dark field!"

"Were you serious about the mice?" I say while staring at the back pockets of his jeans and absolutely nothing else that might be near or underneath them. Definitely not his butt.

"Yes and no. They aren't really something you have to worry about until it gets a little colder. Then you'll find them looking for warm cars to hide in. It's not cold enough for that yet."

The pressure of Jonas's arms wrapped around my legs and the middle of my back while he carries me shuts my mind off in a way that only he can. When he touches me, it feels like I'm borrowing his nervous system for a minute, giving mine a much-needed break.

As effortlessly as he picked me up and carried me, he sets me down in front of the glass doors of his apartment complex.

"Did you do that just so I would look at your butt?" I feel my face heat with embarrassment at the mention of Jonas's butt, which makes me feel about seven years old.

"I did that because you spent twelve hours in a car just to see me, and I'm not going to stand there and watch you try and run away." Fair enough.

"So it's not even *a little bit* about your butt?"

"Elyse—are you okay? Why did you run like that?"

"If I tried to explain it, it wouldn't make any sense."

"I feel like it might make more sense than you sprinting away from me. Are you scared of me?"

"NO. God, no! Not even close! Oh my god. I just...I panicked. You're so beautiful and you smell so nice and that white sweater is insane, like, you look...you could actually be a model."

His face warms with a hint of a smile. The confusion in his expression melts into a softness that tells me he's relieved I still feel safe with him.

"I panicked and I ran away because I think I'm scared you're going to figure out you don't actually like me as much as you think you do. And also, I'm really nervous to kiss you for the first time." I could stand here for a few hours and give Jonas a college-level dissertation on all the reasons I ran away, but I stop myself from saying more. More would be way too much. More would scare him away.

"About the first thing you said." Jonas tugs the strings of his maroon hoodie that I'm wearing and pulls me a tiny bit closer than I was before. "That's never going to happen." He says it so certainly that I have no choice but to believe him. He still hasn't let go of the strings on ~~his~~ my hoodie. He continues: "I don't think you fully understand how *much* I like you and how long I've liked you. I am *in love* with you. The day I met you in Coles—do you know what Josh said to me when you and Evan walked away?"

"...Did he make fun of me?"

"Josh said, 'Jeez, why don't you marry her already!' I told him, 'Maybe I will.' I got home and sent you a friend request on Facebook and saw that you were in a relationship, so I let it go. But the entire walk home from the grocery store, I thought about what it would be like to be married to someone like you. After *one* conversation with you. The more I get to know you, the more I fall in love with you. I'm so *beyond* the point of figuring out how I feel about you. I know how I feel about you. I love you."

I'm trying to keep my expression neutral as I *will* the tears trying to escape from my eyeballs back into my body. "Hearing you say you love me in real life is so different than over FaceTime."

Everything that's happened between us has felt completely upside down and backward. The typical milestones that come with being in a relationship have happened so out of order for us that sometimes it feels silly to even *try* to make sense of what's happening anymore. I've lived my life with a specific kind of rigidity that causes my mind to have a difficult time wrapping itself around what's happening between me and Jonas.

Nothing makes sense.

Our first phone call lasted six hours and happened when we were seven thousand miles apart.

We told each other we loved each other before our first date.

And then our first date lasted *five days*, the first of which I met his entire family and slept in his childhood home.

Three months ago I'd said to Jonas, *"Goodbye forever! I'll never see you again!"* It was the last day of school, and I was trying to squeeze past him to get to my friends.

And now I'm standing in front of him as his girlfriend of—oh, I don't know—*fourteen seconds*? And he's telling me that the very first time we talked, he thought about *marrying me*. I love this man so much, I'm completely sure of that. It's just everything else that feels impossible to understand.

Because it's not supposed to be this easy, is it?

From what I know about love, it crushes you. Whether it's the weight of settling, or the weight of begging to be loved by someone who promised you the world and then disappeared, or the weight of needing to be Someone's Everything All Of The Time—it crushed me all the same.

Nothing about being loved by Jonas feels remotely close to being crushed. In fact, it might be the safest feeling I've ever felt.

"I'm not going anywhere, Elyse. I'm just gonna keep running after you until you tell me not to."

I conveniently forgot how this conversation started—with me running away.

He tugs at the strings of my hoodie and brings me even closer to him. "And about the second thing..." he says directly into my mouth, just loud enough to not be considered a whisper, "I don't know how to break this to you, but we've already kissed."

"It's not the same thing! You're my *boyfriend* now. It's *totally* different."

His mouth is close to mine, but it's clear Jonas is waiting for me to remove the fraction of distance that remains between our lips. I know we're supposed to kiss...I mean, his face is *right there.*

Oh my god, he's right there.

I wrap my arms around him and throw my face into his chest. I borrow his quiet and calm energy and take a deep inhale of his cologne, just because I can. Because he's not a picture or a video or a text in my phone. He really is *right there.*

And he didn't even forget about me.

When I'm hiding inside his arms, which are wrapped all the way around me, I remember our almost-first-kiss in his basement.

"Can I kiss you?"

"You promised me you wouldn't."

I don't know how long we stay locked into our hug, but it's long enough to make my face sweat from my own breath as I exhale into Jonas's soft sweater. As if Jonas can read my mind, he asks quietly into the top of my head, "Can I kiss you?"

I know if I open my mouth and try to speak, I *will* ruin this moment. And I really don't want to ruin this moment. I decide silence is the best option. I lift my chin up to meet his eyeline and I keep my arms wrapped tightly around him.

After waiting twelve hours, and two months, and also my entire life, Jonas kisses me for the very first time as my *boyfriend.* He doesn't know it, but for the second time, he is kissing me as the person I know I want to spend the rest of my life with.

Maybe I will.

A Very Short Novel (& Its Sequel)

The first page of every journal she was gifted and every notebook she saved up to buy all started with the same sentiment: These are the pages that I'm going to write my first book in.

Whether she was *capable* of writing a book was never a question. It was only a matter of time before she got every word out onto the pages and created something beautiful for others to read. *I'll just start by writing a novel and go from there,* she would think.

How hard could it be?

The Very First Novel She Ever Wrote was going to be a raving success. She was absolutely sure of it. So it's curious that when she sat down to write it, nothing ever came out. Never mind that she didn't have a clue about choosing a premise, outline development, character lists, scene blocking, or anything else that one might do before writing the very thing she would write with extreme ease.

She was thirteen years old and more confident than she had any business being, given that she didn't have a single clue what she was doing.

That's *exactly* as confident as a thirteen-year-old should be.

She has never been that confident since.

The Very First Novel She Ever Wrote was going to pour out of her so quickly that she would barely have time to catch it all with her hands and place it into the empty pages of her notebooks. She was going to write The Very First Novel She Ever Wrote with a neon-blue gel pen, of course. She didn't have frequent access to a computer, and whenever she *did*, she was too nervous to ask for permission to use it.

None of that mattered anyway, because she was a writer, which meant she was going to write.

A gel pen and paper would do just fine.

Cynthia packed a VW Bus with her favorite things,
and all her favorite people.
This road trip is going to change her life!

She is running away from home.
She is the only person who knows that.

She was shocked that writing wasn't as easy as she thought it would be. The Very First Novel She Ever Wrote didn't pour out of her. It didn't even trickle out of her. She would have settled for it being surgically removed from her, one word at a time, preferably by her childhood friend Louie, who wouldn't know how to perform a surgery of that magnitude. Mostly because the version of Louie she remembers best is eleven years old, and also, that was just a joke.

She misses Louie very much.

Louie is irrelevant to this story.

The first four sentences of The Very First Novel She Ever Wrote were written into the pages of the fuzzy pink journal she got for Christmas. She also wrote them inside the composition book she bought at 7-Eleven with her allowance. And even in the holographic astronaut spiral notebook from the Scholastic Book Fair, which she loved more than any notebook she's ever purchased.

Cynthia packed a VW Bus with her favorite things,
and all her favorite people.
This road trip is going to change her life!

She is running away from home.
She is the only person who knows that.

A non-comprehensive list of places she started writing The Very First Novel She Ever Wrote:

1. Every notebook she owned.
2. Every journal she was given as a gift.
3. Every ream of blank printer paper she stole from her grandma's computer room and hid under her bed.
4. Every handful of paper napkins she didn't use from fast-food restaurants but held on to just in case.[1]
5. Every extra piece of lined paper her elementary school teachers gave her.[2]
6. Every PalmPilot her dad let her have when his job upgraded his out-of-date technology for a new and improved BlackBerry.[3]
7. Every computer she borrowed.
8. Every computer she owned.
9. Every computer she broke and then sort of fixed because she couldn't afford to buy another computer.
10. Every Word document on every computer listed above.

---

1 She heard once that a well-known author scribbled the outline for her entire book series on a napkin while waiting for a train, so it only made sense that she would do the same.

2 The paper was always so impossibly thin that it ripped every time she tried to erase a mistake or wipe the red smudges left behind from her stained Flamin' Hot Cheeto Fingers.

3 This just happened one time, but writing "The PalmPilot" instead of "Every PalmPilot" would have broken the stream of "Everys" she had going, and it wouldn't have looked as cool. She wants to be cool almost as much as she wants to be a writer.

If I'm meant to be a writer, she would think, *then writing shouldn't feel this impossible.*

Those four sentences lived alone on the first page of so many notebooks, with so many blank pages living beyond, that she began to wonder if they were lonely. If they were judging her. If they resented her. She wondered if they wished they never existed at all.

Sometimes she found herself wishing the very same thing.

But after a while, these four sentences felt less and less like the *first* four sentences and more like the *only* four sentences. As she got older, she realized she hadn't failed at writing a novel at all. The Very First Novel She Ever Wrote was only ever meant to be four sentences long.

Maybe I'll write a sequel that will be longer one day, she thought the night she turned the ages of: eighteen, nineteen, twenty-one, twenty-two.[4]

At twenty-two and three-quarters, she wrote the sequel to Cynthia's story in her journal without meaning to, wanting to, or knowing it at all.

---

4 When she turned twenty years old, she told herself she was content never writing anything ever again. She was lying to herself, obviously, but she couldn't admit that out loud because she didn't know it at the time. She was simply afraid of writing another four-sentence novel.

May 25, 2017

I'm not quite sure when it started, this urgent desire to change everything about my life every so often. An uninvited sadness moves into my chest and grows. Day and night, it grows. Without my permission, it grows. Eventually, it becomes so large and untamed there isn't room for anything else, and I have no other choice but to admit it exists. I allow it to convince me that running away will make me feel better.

Any place will do.
Just as long as it isn't HERE.

On that note... I'm moving to omaha tomorrow. A twelve hour road trip in a car that I don't own, driving to a state I hope will feel like home once I get there. I would promise that I'm not running away this time, but that would be a lie. I'm positive (for no reason at all) that I'll feel way more at home There than any place I've lived before. Maybe I'll feel safe enough to settle down. Maybe I'll even feel like I belong somewhere! Maybe I belong THERE! That would be nice, wouldn't it? Yes, that would be nice.

This morning, I consolidated the few items I own into my two suitcases. One suitcase is ONLY books. Fifty pounds of books. I care more about the books than I do any of my clothes. I have a recurring daydream where I pack all my clothes into my suitcases and then throw them straight into Lake Irving. Just once, I would like to know what it feels like to throw a suitcase into a lake. I should probably keep all my clothes, just in case. Who knows what New Me wears anyway. She might be a skirt person! (though I highly doubt it). I better keep all my clothes just in case.

I want this time to be different.
I <u>need</u> it to be different.
What if it's not any different?

I've convinced everyone I'm leaving behind that I'm making the right decision. Everytime I have conversations like these – The Goodbye Kind – I can tell by the look on people's faces they believe me less and less when I say "this is for the best!" I hear the encouraging words come out of my mouth and I can't help but wonder why it sounds like a stranger is saying them. Who am I even trying to encourage? Them or me?

I'm flooded with equal parts hope and regret. From all my experiences with running away, I've learned there's no place far enough that can grant me the privilege of escaping myself. I've tried so many times. EVERYTHING about me is coming with me tomorrow, whether I like it or not. I need to find a way to make myself feel so overwhelmingly at Home in Omaha that any other hypothetical HERE or THERE doesn't sound as appealing when this unwelcome guest in my chest convinces me it's time to run again.

Wherever I go, there I am.
Here, there, and Always.

She's lived Cynthia's four-sentence story so many times without meaning to. In fact, she'd forgotten about Cynthia entirely until she started writing again. Now, at twenty-two and three-quarters, she has this thought for the very first time: I think I am Cynthia.

Embarrassed to admit that she'd never made that connection before, she creates a Special Edition of The Very First Novel She Ever Wrote in a journal that isn't new, and she didn't buy it for the sole purpose of writing a novel.

Cynthia packed a VW Bus with her favorite things,
and all her favorite people.
This road trip is going to change her life!

She is running away from home.
She is the only person who knows that.

Cynthia drove for quite some time.
Her life changed as much as she wanted,
and changed even more after that.

She got tired of running away from home,
and all that driving didn't excite her the way it used to.

Eventually, Cynthia found home in herself
then she found home in someone else,
and then she learned how to fall in love with

Staying.

Gratitude

First and foremost, I am thankful for YOU, MY DEAR READER!!! Thank you for picking up this book and allowing it into your life. The fact that this book exists and that you're reading it (and considering you've gotten to the acknowledgments, even finished it!) will never lose its impact on me. I hope it encourages you to write your own stories and to be brave as you do.

Thank you to Cassie Jones, my amazing editor, who frequently had to answer anxious questions like "Am I a good enough writer to write a book?" and "Are you absolutely sure I'm a good enough writer to write a book?" and "When you read it, does it read like a real book?" Also, I'm sorry I cried when I met you and tried to explain my creative concept, but I was so excited that I couldn't get the words out so tears came out instead. You've always handled me with as much care as you handled this book.

Thank you to the team at William Morrow/HarperCollins for helping me bring this book into existence. You took a chance on me and supported my creative vision from start to finish. There is so much work that goes on behind the scenes when taking a book from a hypothetical idea to a physical piece

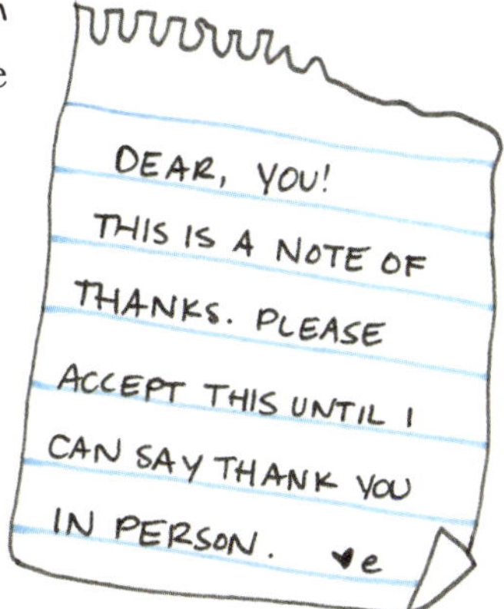

of art someone can hold in their hands and enjoy. From Editorial to Contracts and Legal to Managing Editorial and Production to Design and Art to Marketing and Publicity to Sales and beyond: I hope I get to thank all of you in person one day. Until then, please accept this note of thanks as a placeholder.

Linnea Toney, you are my friend first and my manager second. Thank you for believing in my ability to write long-form stories even before I did. I used to believe your gift was seeing potential in people. The longer I know you, the more I believe I was wrong. You don't just see potential in people; you help those around you believe in themselves. You help people see the greatness that lives in them. Because of that, you helped me dig up a dream I'd buried in fear. I WROTE A BOOK, LINNEA! I REALLY DID IT.

JL Stermer, my literary agent and truly one of the best dressers I know: thank you for walking me through this journey and always knowing the right thing to say when I don't. I couldn't imagine going through this process without you. I can't wait for this book to live on your bookshelf so that when we have our next Zoom meeting, I'll see the spine peeking out among all the other incredible books you've helped bring to life.

To my dear friends Harry Kaufman and YB, thank you for being the first to read this manuscript, for sticking with it before any of the hundreds of typos were removed, and for keeping me sane during the writing and editing process. Your encouragement brought my love for this book back to life when I got to the stage of the Creative Process™ where I decided *this was the worst thing I'd ever created* and *maybe I'm not actually a writer after all.* Trying to create something when filled with self-doubt is like trying to walk through quicksand, and your encouragement was the hand that helped me back to solid ground.

I'd like to thank New York City, because so much of this book was written on the floor of a hotel room while I swung between hyperventilating over an impending deadline and feeling more inspired than I've felt in a long time from walking around and listening to music.

Books—just all books in general—thank you for saving my life.

And finally, to my family.

Jonas Myers, thank you for having so much belief in me. I love you with *everything*. What I am about to write I've told you in private. Still, I will write it here so everyone else knows just how grateful I am for your relentless and unconditional support. You are an incredible stay-at-home father to our two boys. Everything I do is possible because you intentionally release me to dream, to run, to create, and to come home and "show you something cool." You help me believe I am brave, and you help me believe I am capable of great things. When I don't believe I am *either*, you have enough Belief for both of us. You take every chance you can to tell me all the reasons you see me as worthy of so much Belief. Over the course of our last nine years together, your consistent and intentional reminders have rewired my brain to a default setting of: Belief in myself. You truly are a "courageous husband," an "inspiring dad," and a "healthy friend." I am forever changed because I am loved by you.

And to my sons, August and Oliver, thank you for being patient with me while I had to be away from you while bringing this book to life. When you read this one day, I hope the stories in this book solidify how extraordinarily your parents love each other. No matter what happens in life, you can always be sure of that fact. We will always love each other, and we will always love you. All these stories are what led me to you.

things that help me

survive the writing process

the hyperfixation graveyard

crochet
magic
collecting pokémon cards
baking banana bread
web dev
cross stitch
drawing
painting nails
painting
making homemade ice cream
bullet journaling
roller skating
softball
yarn hooking
chicken + zucchini
friendship bracelets

About the Author

Elyse Myers is a writer, comedian, content creator, and host of the podcast *Funny Cuz It's True* who's known to her twelve million followers as "The Internet's Best Friend," sharing relatable stories and comedic sketches and serving as an advocate for topics such as neurodivergence, impostor syndrome, body image, and more. Whether she's making people laugh with stories of disastrous dates or giving a voice to that awkward internal monologue many of us have, she has three simple goals behind everything she makes: to make people feel known, loved, and like they belong. She hopes that by sharing her authentic and unfiltered self with the world, others will feel comfortable doing the same. Elyse lives in the Midwest with her smokeshow of a husband, two sons, and her Pillow Pet named Wallace.

12
9
3
6
PASTA
Face
Touching